HAUNTED
VICTORY

ALSO BY WILLIAM NESTER

THE REVOLUTIONARY YEARS, 1775–1789
The Art of American Power During the Early Republic

THE HAMILTONIAN VISION, 1789–1800
The Art of American Power During the Early Republic

THE JEFFERSONIAN VISION, 1800–1815
The Art of American Power During the Early Republic

HAUNTED VICTORY

THE **AMERICAN** **CRUSADE** TO **DESTROY SADDAM** AND **IMPOSE** **DEMOCRACY** ON **IRAQ**

WILLIAM NESTER

Potomac Books
Washington, D.C.

Library of Congress Cataloging-in-Publication Data
Nester, William R., 1956–
    Haunted victory : the American crusade to destroy Saddam and impose democracy on Iraq / William Nester. — 1st ed.
        p. cm.
    Includes bibliographical references and index.
    ISBN 978-1-59797-944-3 (hardcover : alk. paper)
    ISBN 978-1-59797-945-0 (electronic edition)
    1. Iraq War, 2003– 2. United States—Foreign relations—Iraq. 3. Iraq—Foreign relations—United States. I. Title.
    DS79.76.N47 2012
    956.7044'3—dc23
                                            2011028333

Potomac Books
22841 Quicksilver Drive
Dulles, Virginia 20166

First Edition

10 9 8 7 6 5 4 3 2 1

Contents

ROUND ONE: The Obsession

ROUND TWO: Shock and Awe

ROUND THREE: Cataclysms

Acknowledgments

I cannot express enough my deep gratitude to Elizabeth Demers, my editor at Potomac Books, first for wanting to publish my "Art of American Power" series and then for carefully editing my books. She made numerous corrections and wonderful suggestions that greatly strengthened each one. She is an outstanding professional in her field. I also owe a great deal to Don McKeon and Aryana Hendrawan for their own excellent editing of this manuscript. It is such a great pleasure to work with such wonderful people and professionals as Elizabeth, Don, and Aryana.

Introduction

"You can't distinguish between al-Qaeda and Saddam when you talk about the war on terrorism. They are both equally bad and equally evil and equally destructive. . . . The danger is that al-Qaeda becomes an extension of Saddam's madness and his capacity to extend weapons of mass destruction around the world."

—PRESIDENT GEORGE W. BUSH

"Simply stated, there is no doubt that Saddam Hussein has weapons of mass destruction. There is no doubt that he is massing them to use against our friends, against our allies, and against us."

—VICE PRESIDENT DICK CHENEY

Champions of the Iraq War felt elated and vindicated at the election results announced on March 27, 2010, nearly three weeks after Iraqis went to the polls on March 7. Ayad Allawi's secular, Western-leaning Iraqiya Party won a plurality with 91 seats in the 325-seat parliament, nosing ahead of Nuri Kamal al-Maliki's Islamist, Iran-leaning State of Law Coalition, which garnered 89 seats. This slight majority entitled Allawi to try to form a government and run Iraq.[1]

Any victory celebrations, however, might have been premature. Al-Maliki, the sitting prime minister, denounced the election as fraudulent and declared, "No way we will accept these results." The fiercely anti-American Islamist Moktada al-Sadr, whose Iraqi National Alliance took seventy seats, could not directly be reached for comment—his headquarters has been in Iran since 2007. Indeed, within a week of the election all three parties sent delegations not to Washington, but to Tehran for the blessing of Iran's revolutionary Islamist leadership and advice in brokering a coalition government.

Iraq's second democratic election was held nearly seven years to the day after March 19, 2003, when President George W. Bush barked, "Let's go!" authorizing the conquest of Iraq. In a dazzling display of "shock and awe" military might of America, its junior partner Britain, and eventually contingents from around forty other countries, Iraq's army and government were destroyed within a month. On May 1 President Bush was flown to the USS *Abraham Lincoln*, where, with a huge "Mission Accomplished" banner behind him, he proclaimed that "in the battle of Iraq, the United States and its allies have prevailed." Henceforth the job was to stabilize the country and mop up "deadenders," as those who fought the invaders were derisively called. In December 2003 the dictator Saddam Hussein was captured and would eventually be tried and executed.

Tragically, despite these early coups and the president's triumphant announcement, victory would prove to be elusive. After the shock and awe wore off, an insurgency erupted, and thousands of American troops and tens of thousands of Iraqis died in the fighting. But once again American power eventually prevailed. The turning point came in 2007, when Gen. David Petraeus implemented a "surge" strategy that either co-opted or crushed the insurgents. Along the way, the Americans got Iraq's anti-Saddam leaders to design and implement a democratic political system with a constitution, parliament, elections, and civil rights. In 2008 the American and Iraqi governments signed a treaty whereby the United States would withdraw all its combat troops by December 2011. Could Americans then finally celebrate a mission accomplished?

Undoubtedly some would. But for increasing numbers of Americans, that string of victories was haunted figuratively, and for some literally. From the invasion to the second election, the United States sacrificed in Iraq 4,376 troops killed in action and over 35,000 wounded physically and often psychologically, at an economic loss of nearly $900 billion dollars. By 2010 the worst of the human cost for the United States was past; few casualties were anticipated now that American troops were largely confined to bases and

were being steadily withdrawn. The financial cost, however, would continue
to swell steadily in the years and decades to come. Nobel Prize winner
Joseph Stiglitz and esteemed economist Linda Bilmes crunched the numbers
and estimated that the Iraq War would eventually cost the United States at
least $2 trillion and quite likely as much as $3.5 trillion.[2]

And those were just America's quantifiable human and financial costs.
How is national honor or its desecration measured? Critics condemned the
American crusade in Iraq on both legal and moral grounds. Invading a
country that posed no threat to the United States, humiliating and torturing
prisoners, and imposing revolutionary changes on Iraq all grossly violated
international law. The Pew Institute's annual public opinion surveys of
countries around the world found that anti-Americanism soared after the
invasion.[3]

And what of the costs to Iraqis? Did the American invasion alleviate or
diminish the hardships in their lives?

That Saddam Hussein was among history's most vicious dictators was
unquestionable. In his nearly quarter century in power, his policies led to
two ruinous wars, the deaths of over a million Iraqis, Iranians, Kuwaitis,
and others, as well as crippling United Nations sanctions. The average Iraqi
in 2003 was far worse off than when Saddam seized the presidential palace
in 1979.

But did destroying Saddam and his regime, and imposing a democratic
system on its ruins, justify the conquest's methods? While the exact number
of Iraqis who died since the American invasion will never be known, the
group the Iraq Body Count estimates that from 102,315 to 111,832 Iraqis
died from violence between the March 2003 and August 2011. Estimates
of the economic costs are just as varied and controversial, with figures extending from hundreds of billions of dollars to well over one trillion dollars.
The only clear measure is how Iraqis view what happened in their country:
the vast majority of Iraqis have condemned the American crusade.[4]

Further, most Americans reluctantly or bitterly came to share that view,
according to various surveys. Today two out of three Americans believe that
the United States should never have invaded Iraq. That is a titanic shift in
public opinion. Three out of four Americans supported the American war
when it was launched.[5]

What provoked this political seesaw? The swelling tide of blood and treasure changed the minds of many Americans. As if this were not disturbing enough, scandals erupted over the sadistic humiliation of prisoners at Abu Ghraib and the White House's no-bid contracts that ladled tens of billions of dollars to corporations that were major campaign donors to the Republican Party and that often pocketed the money without even starting (let alone finishing) the reconstruction projects.[6]

And atop all this was the sickening realization that the Bush administration at best misrepresented, and at worst outright lied, to justify its war in Iraq. Most Americans had believed President George W. Bush, Vice President Dick Cheney, Defense Secretary Donald Rumsfeld, Secretary of State Colin Powell, National Security Adviser Condoleezza Rice, and countless other prominent, zealous public figures within and beyond the White House when they repeatedly insisted that Iraq was allied with Al Qaeda, was partly to blame for the September 11 attacks, and posed an imminent threat to the United States with its weapons of mass destruction (WMDs). Eventually each of those assertions was exposed as false.

Although public opinion has shifted over whether the Iraq War was justified, three perspectives have persisted. Conservatives grounded their support for a war against Iraq on three beliefs: (1) Iraq was behind September 11, (2) Iraq was massing weapons of mass destruction to attack the United States, and (3) the destruction and replacement of Saddam's dictatorship with a democracy would inspire democratic revolutions across the Arab and Islamic worlds. Humanitarians and realists opposed the war for the same broad array of reasons but emphasized different elements. Humanitarians condemned the war because they believed that it would leave the Iraqi people worse off, realists because it would damage American wealth, power, security, and honor.

In addition, realists dismissed all three conservative beliefs as either untrue or irrelevant. They understood that Saddam had no connection with the September 11 attacks and actually was the enemy of Osama bin Laden and Al Qaeda. They knew that Iraq's nuclear weapons program was destroyed but assumed that Saddam had some fragments of his former chemical weapons and possibly biological weapons programs hidden away. If so, these weapons were most likely not operational. Even if they were, Saddam would be deterred from using them knowing that the United States and its allies would destroy him and his regime in retaliation. He would only use WMDs if the United States and its allies invaded Iraq. Finally, the realists predicted that destroying Saddam's regime would bring a Shiite, pro-Iranian government to power in Iraq, while free elections elsewhere across the Middle East and beyond would likely result not in pro-Western liberal democracies but anti-Western Islamist revolutions. Instead, the realists insisted that their triple containment strategy toward Iraq promoted American and Western security at a very low annual cost of a billion or so dollars. Under that strategy, the United States and United Nations contained Iraq, and Iraq in turn contained Islamism within Iraq and neighboring Iran. The result was a stable power balance in the Persian Gulf between two enemies, the secular Arab Sunni regime in Iraq and the Islamist Persian Shiite revolutionary regime in Iran.

This book explores the dynamic trajectory of beliefs, actions, and consequences that will forever be debated as among the most controversial and costly to American security, power, wealth, and honor in the nation's history. While many other books have appeared on the Iraq War, this is the first that comprehensively unveils the moral dilemmas that entangled the Bush administration and the American public through each stage of planning, selling, fighting, and ending the war. At the book's heart are the vivid revelations of the behind-the-scenes policy tugs-of-war over whether to go to war against Iraq and, if so, how to fight that war.

ROUND ONE:
THE OBSESSION

"The threat posed by Iraq is crucial to winning the war on terror. . . . We cannot wait for the final proof, the smoking gun, that could come in the form of a mushroom cloud."
—GEORGE W. BUSH

"Deliverable weapons of mass destruction in the hands of a terror network, or a murderous dictator, or the two working together constitute as grave a threat as can be imagined."
—DICK CHENEY

"No terrorist state poses a greater or more immediate threat to the security of our people than the regime of Saddam Hussein and Iraq."
—DONALD RUMSFELD

"What new information exits? What threat can be quantified? What has changed in recent months or years? How much will it cost? If we change regimes, who will be in the new regime and has that been thought through?"
—SEN. TOM DASCHLE

"It's nice to say we can do it unilaterally, except we can't."
—COLIN POWELL TO GEORGE W. BUSH

"Mr. President, do not rush to war."
—SEN. JOHN KERRY

"The streets in Basra and Baghdad are sure to erupt in joy."
—DICK CHENEY

1
The Legacy

The Iraq War, which began with the American-led invasion on March 19, 2003, and sputters on through today, is a result of an explosive mix of historical geopolitical animosities and conservative ideological obsessions. Iraq has been an American foreign policy problem ever since Saddam Hussein ordered his army to brutally conquer Kuwait on August 2, 1990. Americans cheered George H. W. Bush's brilliant diplomacy, which in six months forged an international coalition of 550,000 troops from twenty-seven nations that routed Iraq's army from Kuwait, a conflict that came to be known as the Gulf War. That war's ending, however, enraged conservatives. The president abruptly ordered the coalition's forces to cease fire before they completely encircled and destroyed the elite Republican Guard divisions that were the backbone of Saddam's power. Conservatives argued that Saddam most likely would have been overthrown had Bush let American armored and airborne divisions eliminate these troops and then race to Baghdad's outskirts. This might have panicked Iraqi generals into turning their guns on their dictator.

Stung by the criticism, Bush then caved before conservative demands that he encourage revolts among southern Shiites and northern Kurds, which might precipitate Saddam's demise. But once again, the president outraged conservatives when he refused to aid the rebels, thus allowing Saddam to launch massive attacks that crushed both revolts.

That was not necessarily bad from a practical point of view. Reasoning that "the devil you know is better than the devil you don't," realists argued that it was better to box in Saddam than to create a power vacuum that might result in Iraq breaking up among Sunni, Shiite, and Kurdish warlords, which in turn would tempt intrigues and possibly outright invasions from neighboring Iran, Syria, and Turkey to protect their respective interests.

Thus, from the end of the Gulf War until March 19, 2003, Washington followed a triple containment policy toward Iraq: the United States and the United Nations worked together to contain Saddam's regime, and Saddam in turn brutally suppressed Islamism within Iraq and contained neighboring Iran, with its revolutionary Islamist government. This strategy was initially a dazzling success. Under UN auspices inspectors rooted out and destroyed hundreds of tons of chemical and biological weapons, and dismantled a nuclear program that was only half a year shy of producing a bomb. These inspections were backed by economic sanctions and "no-fly zones" over northern and southern Iraq. This containment policy only cost American taxpayers about $1.5 billion a year.

Although Saddam could fume and bluster, the dictator lacked the offensive military power to threaten neighboring countries, let alone the United States. There were periodic minor crises as he tested the resolve of first the Bush and then the Clinton White Houses. Periodically his agents impeded the work of the inspectors and his antiaircraft batteries locked onto American and British warplanes patrolling the no-fly zones. In 1993 he may have gone so far as to dispatch assassins after former president Bush who was visiting Kuwait.[1] The White House responded to each challenge with bombing and missile attacks that stung Saddam into backing off for a while.

With centrist Bill Clinton in the White House, conservatives found someone to hate as much as Saddam. Throughout Clinton's eight years as president, they attacked him not just for continuing the Iraq containment policy, but for virtually everything he did and did not do; indeed, the bitterness of their attacks swelled with the success of his policies. But the conservative obsession with Saddam never abated. In 1998, Donald Rumsfeld, Paul Wolfowitz, and John Bolton—the future president George W. Bush's defense secretary, deputy defense secretary, and under secretary of state for arms control, respectively—along with other leading conservatives wrote a stern public letter to President Clinton blasting his policies as "dangerously inadequate" and demanding that "the only acceptable strategy" was the destruction of Saddam's regime as "the aim of American foreign policy."[2]

And just how would that be done? The conservative "solution" was typically simplistic: unleash the hodgepodge of exiled personalities and groups known as the Iraqi National Congress (INC). It did not matter that the CIA and State Department, which had worked with the INC for years, dismissed as hopelessly naive any notion of using it against Saddam's regime. They warned that the INC was corrupt, inept, faction-ridden, brutal, and thoroughly penetrated by Saddam's agents. Worst of all, the INC peddled useless, misleading, and often blatantly false "intelligence."

Nonplussed by the experts' advice, the conservatives in the Republican-dominated Congress drafted the Iraq Liberation Act of 1998, which granted the INC $98 million in military aid and $43 million in political aid to overthrow Saddam. The result was just as CIA and State Department experts predicted. Much of the money was pocketed by corrupt "freedom fighters," while Saddam's agents and soldiers nabbed those few INC agents who tried to infiltrate Iraq. Saddam followed that up in October 1998 by provoking another crisis over inspections. The United Nations agreed to a request by President Clinton and Prime Minister Tony Blair to withdraw the inspectors so that the United States and Britain could retaliate. But a three-day bombing campaign in December failed to force Saddam to reaccept the disarmament program. Thus Iraq was inspection-free from late 1998 until late 2002. All along, conservatives were unrelenting in attacking the containment policy.

The conservative obsession with destroying Saddam's regime offended American humanitarians and realists alike. Both recognized that the Gulf War, compounded by UN sanctions and inspections, had destroyed Iraq's military power to threaten others. Thus that obsession with Iraq distracted American policymakers from dealing with an array of genuine threats to American security, including Al Qaeda, the soaring national debt, and global warming, to name the most prominent. Humanitarians and realists, however, parted ways over sanctions. Humanitarians argued that the sanctions should be revoked since they only hurt the Iraqi people. Realists wanted smart sanctions that hurt the regime but not the average Iraqi.

There is irony in the conservative campaign against Saddam Hussein. After all, the dictator they condemned as a monster since August 1990 had been a hero of sorts to them during the 1980s. Saddam remained a painfully embarrassing reminder of the utter failure of the collaborationist policy toward Iraq that was upheld by presidents Ronald Reagan and George H. W. Bush from December 1983 until August 1990. Indeed, Rumsfeld initiated this policy on December 23, 1983, when he flew to Baghdad and shook hands with Saddam. In a classic remake of the "Frankenstein syndrome," Reagan and Bush boosted Saddam's power with a plethora of military, economic, and intelligence windfalls that he would eventually use against Kuwait.

What was the motivation? From a realist perspective, the policy did make sense at the time. Iraq then was believed to be the lesser of two evils when compared with Iran, whose Islamist revolution in 1979 had toppled the shah, an American ally; invaded the U.S. embassy; held fifty-two Americans captive for 444 days; and helped topple Jimmy Carter's presidency. Although Iraq had been a Soviet client state since the socialist Ba'ath Party took power in a blood-soaked coup in 1963, an opportunity arose to pull Iraq Westward and undermine Iran. That chance came in 1980 when Saddam launched a war against Iran for control of the Shatt al-Arab waterway, a war that was also a secular assault on Islamic fundamentalism. The war quickly bogged down into a stalemate that ground on until the 1988 armistice. By aiding Iraq openly and Iran secretly, the Reagan administration sought to vent the passions of each against the other while gaining influence over both. This was a sound policy in theory, similar superficially to President Richard Nixon's strategy of playing off the Soviets and Chinese against each other by pursuing détente with both.

But some unanticipated problems arose. First, Reagan and his men committed an array of felonies known as the Iran-Contra scandal, which eventually was revealed, investigated, and prosecuted. Although Reagan escaped impeachment for political rather than legal reasons—Democrats irrationally feared that hounding another law-breaking president from office a decade after Nixon would harm rather bolster American democracy—fourteen of his underlings were indicted and eleven convicted. But the policy did not just violate the Constitution and an array of federal laws—it grossly undermined American national security.

The Cassandras were right all along: collaborating with Iraq would sooner or later end disastrously for the United States. That prediction came true on August 2, 1990. And thereafter the conservatives sought vengeance, ironically for a tragic series of events stemming from their own excesses, follies, and delusions.

2

Thwarted Dreams

From the day that George W. Bush took the oath of office, he and most of his inner circle were obsessed with overthrowing Saddam Hussein. Paul O'Neill, the treasury secretary, later recalled his bafflement that toppling the dictator was a topic, let alone a priority, of the first National Security Council (NSC) meeting on January 30, 2001, and then of the second meeting a few days later. Rumsfeld led the conservatives in arguing that a war against Iraq "would demonstrate what U.S. policy is all about" and assert American hegemony over the Middle East.[1]

The conservatives were confident that with Bush in the White House and other ideological soul mates dominating Congress, the courts, and the bureaucracy, they would soon fulfill their dreams of a free Iraq as well as a range of other heartfelt obsessions. Yet, as with so many other issues, the Bush team's zealotry on Iraq collided with the complexities and paradoxes of the real world. Although they swiftly enacted much of the conservative agenda into law and policy, they found that demanding Saddam's overthrow was much easier than realizing it.

Nonetheless, the conservatives forged blindly ahead. After all, they could always play the blame game. Long after he left office, Bill Clinton remained the conservative whipping boy, along with everything else that they believed was wrong with the world. But this political tactic only worked with fellow conservatives. Having taken over all three branches of government, the ideologues now faced the same potential criticisms that they had hurled against the Clinton White House.

So just how would Saddam be overthrown? Before September 11, George W. Bush and his teammates could only fume in frustration. Paul Wolfowitz led those who groped for any excuse to launch a second war against Iraq, a war they somehow hoped to initiate by pumping money into the INC's coffers. He was the point man for an ideological spearhead that included Cheney, Rumsfeld, Cheney's chief of staff Lewis "Scooter" Libby, and Under Secretary of State for Arms Control John Bolton. National Security Adviser Rice was reputedly a half-hearted member of this coterie. Beyond the White House, calls for war against Iraq were cheered by the spectrum of right-wing publications and groups, with the *Wall Street Journal*, the *Weekly Standard*, American Enterprise Institute, and the Defense Policy Board the shrillest voices.

But not everyone in the Bush administration was so trigger-happy. Secretary of State Powell led a handful of realists—his deputy Richard Armitage, CIA Director George Tenet, counterterrorist chief Richard Clarke, envoy to the Israeli-Palestinian peace talks retired general Anthony Zinni, and Treasury Secretary Paul O'Neill—who argued that American security was best served by maintaining the containment policy, with its relatively low diplomatic, military, economic, and moral costs. When asked if Saddam worried him, Powell replied, "I do not lose a lot of sleep about him late at night."[2]

Powell's realism was backed by powerful voices both foreign and American. In January 2001 the governments of Turkey, Jordan, and Saudi Arabia greeted George W. Bush's inauguration by expressing their scorn for the INC and urging the neophyte president not to let the exiles kick over a hornet's nest in Iraq. That message was echoed at home in a letter to the president by a group of high-ranking former intelligence, defense, and foreign policy experts.[3]

Yet, given its low feasibility, the press of other issues, and the realist opposition, the notion of overthrowing Saddam fell far down the priority list. While the INC's bank accounts swelled with White House–directed aid, history repeated itself just as the realists had predicted. Most of the money merely made the Iraqi exile leaders richer; little was used against Saddam.

In August 2001 the INC's television station began broadcasts from London, set up with a $1 million grant and further funded with $1.3 million in annual operating costs. Learning of abuses, the State Department withheld the rest of the grant pending an audit over just how the INC had spent the money.[4]

For now the only other thing Bush could do was to step up the bombing campaign against Iraq. Saddam gave him the perfect excuse to do so. In 2000 the Iraqis either locked onto allied warplanes with radar or actually fired 221 times in the southern zone and 145 times in the northern zone, which led to forty-eight and nineteen days, respectively, of retaliatory bombing. During Bush's first six months in office the number of incidents leaped to 370 and 62 in the southern and northern zones, which provoked thirty-two and seven days of counterattacks in those zones. All the conservative chest-thumping had clearly not intimidated Saddam.[5]

The largest strikes occurred on February 17, when Bush authorized two dozen American and British warplanes to attack five targets around Baghdad after weeks of Iraqi antiaircraft sties locking on with radar or firing at allied warplanes. When asked about the attacks, Bush declared that "Saddam Hussein has got to understand that we expect him to conform to the agreement he signed after Desert Storm. We will enforce the no-fly zone, both south and north."[6]

Bush's comments revealed his ignorance of the Iraq problem. Michael O'Hanlon, a Brookings Institution expert, pointed out that "the president seemed to merge different concepts in his head in a random and somewhat illogical way. I didn't get a sense he had a real clear grasp in his own mind of exactly what yesterday's strike was about."[7] What the president failed to comprehend was that the agreement Saddam had signed established the international inspection regime to dismantle his WMDs. Bush senior belatedly ordered no-fly zones set up in the north in March 1991 and the south in August 1992, supposedly to aid revolts by the Kurds and Shiites, respectively. But he abandoned both of those rebellions to slaughter by the Iraqi army. The UN Security Council never authorized the zones that Bush had ordered.

A range of countries condemned the bombing war. NATO members France and Turkey protested the raids for provoking rage in the "Arab street" and thus undermining moderate Arab states. Egyptian president Hosni Mubarak declared that the bombings did nothing but "kill innocent people." The Arab League, Moscow, and Beijing made their own protests.

Setting aside questions over the legality of the no-fly zones, the mismatch in military power was clear enough. Of all the missiles the Iraqis fired, only one may have hit its target. The Pentagon would not say whether an un-manned Predator spy drone was shot down or crashed from a mechanical failure in July 2001. That same month, an Iraqi antiaircraft missile almost hit a U-2 spy plane flying at 60,000 feet. But in return, American and British warplanes pounded parts of Iraq's air defense system to rubble.

While persisting in his self-destructive challenge in the no-fly zones, Saddam tried something else: he played the "oil card." With 112 billion bar-rels of petroleum locked beneath its sands, Iraq had 16.4 percent of the world's known oil reserves, second only to Saudi Arabia's 38.2 percent, or 259.3 billion, and ahead of Kuwait's 94.0 billion, Iran's 89.7 billion, and Venezuela's 77.9 billion. But Iraq supplied only 11.7 percent of world oil exports, compared to Saudi Arabia's 38.4 percent. Only one of three Iraqi oil fields was active.[8]

Ironically, despite all the Bush team's bluster, no country bought more Iraqi oil than the United States. In April 2002, of Iraq's daily average oil ex-ports of 1.25 million barrels, the United States imported 878,330 barrels, or two-thirds of the total, compared to Europe's 334,583, Canada's 74,250, Japan's 18,083, and South Korea's 8,500. In all, Iraq accounted for about 8 percent of America's oil imports.[9]

The hypocrisy did not end there. Like his predecessors, Bush turned a blind eye to the massive smuggling of $1 billion of oil a year across Iraq's borders with Turkey, Syria, Jordan, and Iran. America's NATO ally Turkey smuggled from 40,000 to 150,000 barrels of Iraqi oil and diesel fuel a day through its territory to foreign markets. This, however, made up only a frac-tion of the $30 billion that Turkey had lost to trade since the trade sanctions were imposed on Iraq. Because the Americans used the U.S. Air Force base at Incirlick to patrol Iraq's skies, Bush's administration, like Clinton's, did not pressure Ankara to curb the smuggling. From November 2000 Baghdad sold Damascus low-priced oil that was shipped through the 552-mile pipeline that stretches to the Syrian port of Banias on the Mediterranean.

That volume reached up to 150,000 barrels a day. With no love lost between Washington and Damascus, the Bush team fruitlessly tried to get the Syrians to shut the spigot. Indeed, the marketing of Iraqi petroleum beyond the Security Council's "oil for food" program was so blatant that "smuggling" did not properly describe it. In January 2001 Egypt, Syria, and Jordan openly signed trade agreements with Iraq, while Turkey upgraded its relationship to the ambassadorial level. In response to all this, conservatives could only smolder at the contradictions, hypocrisies, and impotencies of the Iraq policy.[10]

Saddam tried to capitalize on the Bush team's policy schizophrenia and America's oil dependence in April 2001 when he withdrew shipments to the United States and demanded that other OPEC members follow suit. It was a futile and self-defeating gesture. Rival producers took advantage of the short spike in oil prices by signing new long-term contracts. Before the month's end, Saddam resumed payments. The United States had alternative sources of supply, while Iraq could not find new buyers.

But Saddam's brief embargo did spark a renewed debate over the efficacy and morality of the international economic sanctions on Iraq, which were determined by fourteen UN Security Council resolutions and subsequent oversight. Under the 1996 "oil-for-food" deal between the Security Council and Saddam, Iraq could sell about two million barrels of oil a day. Profits from the sales accrued to an UN escrow account that was deducted for Iraqi purchases of an approved list of goods, including food, medicine, and other humanitarian products; a portion of these oil revenues went to Kuwait as reparations. The list was reviewed every six months. Each permanent Security Council member had veto power over any contract between Iraq and another country. The United States had frequently wielded this power to block questionable items on the list, $5 billion worth in 2001 alone. Despite this scrutiny Saddam and his cronies found a way to skim at least $1 billion a year off that flow into their own pockets from 1996 to 2002.[11]

For years Paris and Moscow tried to get the Security Council to abolish all sanctions against Iraq. Economic interests were their primary motive. From 1996 through 2001, Russia and France, respectively, sold $4.3 billion and $3.1 billion of goods and services to Iraq. Baghdad still owed Moscow over $8.5 billion in debt racked up during the days when it was still a Soviet client. Russian and French oil firms had invested heavily in Iraq and feared losing those assets in any war. Saddam doled out contracts to those two countries to buy their restraint on the Security Council. In 2001 alone, Saddam awarded $1.3 billion in new contracts to Russian companies and promised $40 billion more if the sanctions were lifted. But Paris and Moscow justified their position by citing statistics on Iraq's child mortality and malnutrition rates, which they joined Baghdad in claiming were the result of the sanctions. In reality the billions of dollars that Saddam and his henchmen stole from the oil-for-food program were more than enough to alleviate Iraq's health problems.[12]

Prime Minister Blair sought compromise between no sanctions and the unwieldy existing system. Secretary of State Powell convinced a reluctant Bush and other White House hardliners to back Blair's initiative to replace the eleven-year trade embargo with a list of prohibited goods and the resumption of arms inspections. On May 30, 2001, the British ambassador to the United Nations announced this proposal to the Security Council. But the plan was shelved when Russia, China, and France opposed any restrictions. Starting on June 12, talks were resumed among the five permanent members but led only to stalemate.

Frustrations swelled among conservatives within and beyond the White House. Saddam Hussein could thumb his nose at America with impunity. But the conservatives would soon find a way to vent their rage and fulfill their dream of destroying Saddam and his regime.

3

Cooking the Books

The turning point in the tug-of-war between the conservatives and realists over Iraq came with the devastating attacks on the World Trade Center and the Pentagon on September 11, 2001. In his book *Against All Enemies*, then counterterrorist chief Richard Clarke revealed that Bush himself was obsessed with finding evidence of an Iraqi connection to the attacks. In the White House's Situation Room on September 12, Bush demanded not once but three times that Clarke and his analysts prove a link: "He grabbed a few of us and closed the door to the conference room. 'Look,' he told us. 'I . . . want you, as soon as you can, to go back over everything. . . . See if Saddam did this. See if he's linked in any way.'" An exasperated Clarke replied that "Al Qaeda did this." That had no effect on Bush. He was adamant that somehow a link be found between Saddam and September 11 even if it did not really exist.[1]

No link was found then or since. That did not stop the conservatives from doing all they could to use September 11 to justify a war against Iraq. During the NSC meetings in the days following the attack, the ideologues pressed for warring against Iraq rather than Al Qaeda. This astounded Clarke and the handful of other realists present, including Powell, Armitage, and Tenet. Clarke was incredulous that the conservatives "were going to try to take advantage of this national tragedy to promote their agenda about Iraq." After days of debate, the realists managed to get Bush to shelve Iraq's fate for now and focus on destroying Al Qaeda.[2]

Enraged by that defeat, the conservatives tried other ways to promote their agenda. During the Bush years, the Defense Policy Board was an eighteen-member private lobby group and advisory body to the Defense Department that periodically met in the conference room beside Rumsfeld's office. On September 19 and 20, the group hosted Ahmed Chalabi, the INC chair, and Khidhir Hamza, the former head of Iraq's nuclear weapons program. The meetings were kept secret from both Secretary Powell and CIA chief Tenet, who viewed Chalabi and the INC as liabilities rather than assets in the struggle against Saddam.

After nineteen hours of talks, the Defense Policy Board enthusiastically agreed that Iraq should be among the first targets of any retaliation for September 11 and that the United States should invade southern Iraq and set up the INC as an alternative government to Saddam's regime. It then used every political gambit at its disposal to push that policy. Defense Policy Board member Newt Gingrich spoke for the group by asserting that "if we don't use this as the moment to remove Saddam after we replace the Taliban, we are setting the stage for disaster." Gingrich did not elaborate what he meant by disaster. Wolfowitz called for mass-bombing Iraq and then invading the south to seize oil fields around Basra; the United States would sell the oil to finance the INC's efforts to depose Saddam. Rumsfeld pressed the case for attacking Iraq with the "logic" that "there were no decent targets for bombing in Afghanistan" so "we should consider bombing Iraq." Unbeknownst to Powell, John Negroponte, the ambassador to the United Nations, presented a White House statement to the Security Council reserving America's "right to attack" unnamed others. A senior official described Powell as "surprised to find out about it and . . . quite distressed. . . . Somebody should have called him." The *Weekly Standard* led the chorus of conservative publications beating ever louder the drum for war against Iraq. When asked whether his administration was trying to provoke a war with Saddam, Bush rather disingenuously replied, "There's no question that the leader of Iraq is an evil man . . . and so we're watching him very carefully."[3]

An intriguing report made public in October boosted the case for war against Iraq. The Czech government claimed that Mohammad Atta, September 11's ringleader, had met with Ahmed Khalil Ibrahim Samir al-Anil, an Iraqi intelligence officer, in Prague on April 8, 2001. Was Atta being instructed by or reporting to the Iraqis? It was only after months of investigation that the Czech government determined that Atta had never visited Prague. When asked, the FBI confirmed that in fact Atta had been in Florida at the time of the alleged meeting. But by the time that mystery was solved, countless Americans believed that Saddam was behind September 11, and they were disinterested in hearing evidence that refuted this belief. President Bush and his fellow conservatives had done and would continue to do everything possible to propagate that myth.[4]

In the face of this onslaught, Powell was able to maintain the realist position for only so long. On November 21, a little more than two months after September 11, Bush asked Rumsfeld to prepare for the invasion of Iraq. As an excuse to go to war, Bush issued on November 26 an ultimatum to Saddam demanding that he restore international inspections of Iraq's suspected WMD sites. He did not say what he would do if the Iraqi leader remained defiant. He did, however, widen his definition of terrorism in a net that he hoped would snare Iraq. Bush argued that "if anyone harbors a terrorist, they're terrorists. If they fund a terrorist, they're a terrorist. If they house terrorists, they're terrorists. . . . If they develop weapons of mass destruction that will be used to terrorize nations, they will be held accountable."[5]

That so troubled UN Secretary-General Kofi Annan that he spoke out, appropriately, when he was in Oslo to receive his Nobel Peace Prize. He warned the Bush White House that "any attempt or any decision to attack Iraq today will be unwise and could lead to a major escalation in the region." On December 19 he repeated this warning to the White House while urging Baghdad to comply with inspections.[6]

The swelling chorus for war with Iraq deeply worried America's allies in the war against Al Qaeda. British officials were scathing about the attempts of the Bush team ideologues to extend the war against Al Qaeda to Iraq. Their intelligence sources uncovered no evidence linking the September 11 attacks to Iraq. One ranking official rather scornfully suggested, "I know it's a common right-wing view in Washington that Iraq must be involved. But it's a big jump in logic and to go bomb Iraq for this attack would be daft. We need to deal with the job in hand first, Osama bin Laden and his organization, Afghanistan and its future."[7]

The Bush team ratcheted up its rhetorical war against Iraq with the State of Union Address of January 31, 2002. The president linked Iraq, Iran, and North Korea in an "axis of evil" in hopes of rallying American and foreign opinion to what he claimed was the greatest threat to world peace since the fascism and imperialism of Germany, Japan, and Italy during the 1930s and 1940s.

While his fellow true believers thrilled at those words, knowing listeners either smiled wryly or hooted openly. Once again the conservatives had paraded their ignorance of contemporary and more distant history. The notion of an "axis of evil" was puzzling to say the least. Iraq and Iran were mutual enemies, and the links to North Korea with either were tenuous at best, although Pyongyang had at times sold missile technology to Tehran. As if that misinformation were not bad enough, the speechwriters apparently did not consider the intervening half century of America's cold war against the Soviet Union and communism, all along overshadowed by the chance of nuclear Armageddon, as significant enough to warrant mention.

Opposition to the conservative crusade against Iraq began to swell. Neither humanitarians nor realists had taken seriously the Bush team's bellicose rumblings during its first nine months in power. Saddam's ruthless rule appeared to be unshakeable; the opposition groups were too fragmented, miniscule, corrupt, inept, and intimidated to threaten him. Nothing short of a massive American invasion could topple Saddam, which itself seemed an impossible conservative dream.

Then came September 11. Realists and humanitarians were aghast that the conservatives would call for attacking Iraq, which had had nothing to do with September 11, rather than destroying Al Qaeda, the perpetrator of the horrors along with its host in Afghanistan, the Taliban. Word filtered out of the Faustian deal struck by the handful of White House realists with the predominant conservatives. Afghanistan would be invaded first, followed by Iraq. That policy became increasingly evident as 2002 unfolded. The axis-of-evil theme of the president's State of the Union address in January was the first clear indicator. This unleashed the floodgates on a rising torrent of statements and speeches identifying a worsening Iraqi threat that had to be destroyed. Humanitarians and realists began to speak out against any notion of a war against Iraq.

Through August 2002 the handful of moderate congressional Republicans joined with Democrats in trying to restrain the swelling political and ideological tide for war. As Vietnam veterans, realists, and senators, Arizona's John McCain and Nebraska's Chuck Hagel bucked their own party to repeatedly state that the Bush administration had failed to make a convincing case for war. Republican senator Richard Lugar of Indiana, a foreign relations expert, echoed those arguments. While the positions of those three otherwise conservative senators were not surprising given their knowledge and experiences, House Majority Leader Dick Armey's opposition did raise eyebrows. Armey, usually among Congress's more conservative zealots, actually warned that an unprovoked invasion of Iraq would violate international law.[8]

Joining those voices were prominent leaders from previous Republican White Houses such as Henry Kissinger, Brent Scowcroft, and James Baker, who warned that a war against Iraq without the approval of Congress or the Security Council, and without first resolving the Israeli-Palestinian conflict, would exacerbate anti-Americanism around the world, worsen political instability and violence across the Middle East, swell the ranks of Islamist and related terrorist groups, and encourage terrorist attacks. The public warnings of Scowcroft and Baker were especially intriguing because both were close friends of George H. W. Bush and thus may not have voiced these worries without the former president's blessing.

The conservatives' lust for war against Iraq faced legal as well as political obstacles. The Constitution's Article I, Section 8 gives Congress the sole power to declare war. Under the UN Charter, a country can go to war only with Security Council approval under Chapter VII or in self-defense under Article 51.

At first the conservatives asserted that they were unbound by either the Constitution or UN Charter. Through the summer of 2002, the Bush team dismissed any notion of asking Congress to approve their campaign against Iraq. Turning the Constitution inside out, they insisted that the president's role as commander in chief empowered him do whatever he wanted in the name of "defense." As for the United Nations, the conservatives had nothing but contempt for its international laws and institutions.

The Bush team spurned approval from Congress and the United Nations from more than just ideologically driven abhorrence. The conservatives were

trapped in a catch-22 over their charges against Iraq. Hard information dis-
appeared when the UN inspection teams departed Iraq in 1998. Yet the
Bush administration refused to ask the CIA for a national intelligence estimate (NIE) on Iraq. The reason was simple: the preliminary CIA reports
concluded that Iraq posed no offensive threat to its neighbors, let alone the
United States. So rather than ask for a comprehensive analysis that would
only bolster the case for the highly successful containment policy, the Bush
team muzzled the CIA, even trying to censor the testimonies of Director
Tenet and other agency spokespersons before congressional committees.

Instead, conservative leaders publicly declared their assumptions as truth.
Vice President Cheney's assertion before the Veterans of Foreign Wars on
August 26, 2002, was typical: "Simply stated, there is no doubt that Saddam
Hussein now has weapons of mass destruction. There is no doubt he is
amassing them to use against our friends, against our allies, and against us."[9]

Meanwhile the conservatives managed to marginalize the handful of realists within the White House. They prevented Powell, Armitage, and Tenet
from even putting their case on the NSC agenda. The only chance Powell
had of swaying Bush was in a private encounter. He was finally granted one
on August 6, 2002. "It's nice to say we can do it unilaterally," the secretary
of state told the president, "except you can't." Powell warned that a unilateral
war against Iraq that violated both the Constitution and international law
would undermine the war against terrorism and virtually all other American
interests. Although skeptical, Bush agreed to let Powell make his pitch to
the NSC on August 16. The result was a compromise. The United States
would war against Iraq but not alone. Powell would get a Security Council
resolution authorizing a war against Iraq.[10]

But the conservatives had no sooner grudgingly agreed to that deal when
they began trying to kill it. At first Bush typically floated along with the conservative tide. But then, faced with a swelling chorus of prominent
Republican voices defending the Constitution, he flip-flopped. On August
28, Bush declared that he might seek some sign of support from Congress,
although he also insisted that if necessary the United States would war
against Iraq without Security Council approval.[11]

All along the Bush team was dead set on "proving" by any means, fair or
foul, that Iraq had WMDs and Al Qaeda links. The Bush team may have

searched in vain for "smoking gun" evidence to justify its war against Iraq, but plenty of evidence eventually surfaced to reveal all the machinations and deceptions that the administration wielded to sell that very war. When hard evidence proved to be elusive, the Bush team simply fabricated what did not exist.

Among the most damning revelations to later surface that the Bush administration peddled lies to justify war against Iraq was the so-called Downing Street Memo, which was dated July 23, 2002, nearly eight months before the American-led invasion. The memo was intended for Prime Minister Blair's eyes only but was leaked to the press and published on May 1, 2005. The document summarizes a meeting between Richard Dearlove, the chief of Britain's Secret Intelligence Service (also known as MI6), and the Bush team. Dearlove revealed that the president and his inner circle were determined to skew the intelligence reports to validate an invasion: "Bush wanted to remove Saddam through military action, justified by the conjunction of terrorism and WMD. But the intelligence and facts were being fixed around the policy. . . . The Defense Secretary said that the US had already begun 'spikes of activity' to put pressure on the regime. No decision had been taken, but he thought the most likely timing in US minds for military action to begin was January. . . . It seemed clear that Bush had made up his mind to take military action . . . but the case was thin." Moreover, the Bush team cynically intended to manipulate the Iraq threat "30 days before congressional elections" both to rally support for the war in Congress and to elect more pro-war and conservative candidates to Congress. Finally, the conservative obsession with destroying Saddam's regime meant that there "was little discussion in Washington of the aftermath of military action."[12]

The "evidence" that the Bush administration presented to justify its assertions, and thus the war, was thoroughly cooked. The White House exerted enormous pressure on the CIA to cherry-pick intelligence that would support the case for war. Vice President Cheney visited the CIA headquarters nearly a dozen times to pressure analysts to redouble their efforts to find evidence. In addition, the president authorized Wolfowitz to set up an organization within the Pentagon known as the Office of Special Plans, which was headed by Douglas Feith and charged with mining the raw intelligence in search of any nuggets that would back its case for war against Iraq. Feith's group lasted from September 2002 until June 2003. At Langley these zealous conservative efforts became derisively known as "Feith-based analysis," a take on the Bush team's self-proclaimed "faith-based presidency."[13]

Some key evidence to support the case for war came from sources that were later proved to be false. A captured Al Qaeda agent who was interrogated in Egypt later admitted that he had claimed a link between Osama bin Laden and Saddam just to stop being tortured by the Egyptians under CIA supervision. Money was the motivation for Naji Sabri, Iraq's foreign minister from 2001 until the invasion, to claim that Iraq was developing WMDs; the CIA paid him $100,000 for this misinformation. An Iraqi known as "Curveball" who defected to Germany in 1999 claimed to have been an engineer in a plant that produced chemical weapons; his allegations were later proved to have been lies concocted solely for the ample money he was paid. His codename was appropriately ironic.[14]

Indeed, all of the acclaimed intelligence nuggets turned out to be fool's gold. Yet not surprisingly, the Bush team ignored the swelling mountain of intelligence that overwhelmingly refuted every one of their assertions. The president and his inner circle were aware that Iraq had no WMDs well before the invasion. They also knew the likely consequences of an invasion. A January 2003 CIA report predicted the resultant chaos, anarchy, looting, violence, insurgency, and soaring power of Islamism and Iran if the Bush team tried to conquer Iraq.[15]

Central to Bush's case was the allegation that Iraq was trying to revive its nuclear weapons program. As evidence they cited Iraq's efforts to obtain aluminum centrifuge tubes and 550 metric tons of uranium yellowcake from Niger. Experts proved that both claims were false. The aluminum tubes could not be used to refine yellowcake to weapon-grade levels, and the Iraqis never tried to buy that yellowcake. Not everyone was as easily gulled as Congress and the American public. The International Atomic Energy Agency examined the documents and dismissed them as forgeries. The uranium myth took longer to expose. Nonplussed, the Bush team continued to peddle the same lies.

When this yellowcake rumor surfaced, the CIA sent Joseph Wilson, a former ambassador, to Niger in February 2002 to investigate. Wilson soon discovered that the "evidence" consisted of crude forgeries and fantasies.

The minister whose signature was on the document had not served for over a decade. The document's seal was not remotely related to Niger's official seal. The country lacked the infrastructure of mines and roads to deliver that much yellowcake. The two mines themselves were owned by a consortium of investors from Germany, Japan, France, and Spain who knew nothing about such a deal. In all, not only would such a sale have been impossible to keep secret, it would have been impossible to mine, refine, and transport enough to fulfill the deal.[16]

It was later revealed that the Bush administration had actually asked the CIA to fabricate a letter from Tahir Jalil Habbush, Iraq's intelligence chief, to Saddam, dated July 1, 2001, indicating that Mohammad Atta had been trained by Iraq and that Iraq was buying uranium yellowcake from Niger with an Al Qaeda team. The CIA refused to do so. The Bush administration denied the allegation.[17]

The Bush team claims of links between Saddam and Osama bin Laden utterly baffled the CIA and FBI. An FBI spokesman captured this bafflement in February 2003: "We've been looking at this hard for more than a year, and you known what, we just don't think it's there." Indeed the only known time Iraq might have attempted a terrorist attack against an American was in 1993 when former President George H. W. Bush visited Kuwait. The alleged plot was thwarted when the agents were captured, interrogated, and executed. President Clinton ordered a retaliatory cruise missile attack on Iraq's intelligence agency. Otherwise, the only clear aid Saddam provided terrorists was the over $35 million he had awarded in $10,000 grants to the families of Palestinians with a member killed fighting the Israelis and $25,000 to the families of suicide bombers.[18]

The 9/11 Commission would debunk the myth of an Iraq–Al Qaeda link. It concluded that while there were sporadic contacts between low-level Iraqi officials and Al Qaeda agents, there was absolutely no collaboration on the September 11 terrorist attacks or any others. How significant then was the fact that Al Qaeda agents moved though and at times resided in Iraq? Just because terrorists find refuge in a country does not mean that they do so with the government's knowledge, let alone approval and active support. After all, hundreds of foreign terrorists have passed through or lived in the United States despite all government efforts to apprehend them.[19]

The Bush team likewise failed in a strenuous effort to link Iraq to the anthrax attacks on America in late September 2001, which killed five. Once again the evidence did not carry the claim. The anthrax was concocted in an American, not foreign, laboratory. The two primary targets of the attacks— senators Tom Daschle and Patrick Leahy, both Democratic centrists—aroused venomous hatred from America's far right rather than foreigners. But the Bush team certainly did not want to reveal such terrorist attacks by their own ideological allies.[20]

In sum, the justifications for the conservative crusade in Iraq rested on two related false assertions. First, that Iraq had WMDs with which it was planning to attack the United States. Second, that Iraq had conspired with Al Qaeda for the September 11 attacks. There was no smoking gun for either allegation—only boilerplate conservative smoke, mirrors, fervor, and wishful thinking.

4

The Blank Check

In September 2002 the Bush administration launched a massive concerted effort to convince the public that Iraq was behind September 11 and posed an imminent threat to attack the United States with WMDs. Vice President Cheney declared on August 26, that "many of us are convinced that Saddam will acquire nuclear weapons fairly soon." He went on to argue that "deliverable weapons of mass destruction in the hands of a terror network, or a murderous dictator, or the two working together constitute as grave a threat as can be imagined." President Bush stepped before the UN General Assembly on September 12, 2002, and insisted that Iraq "is a grave and gathering danger." Defense Secretary Rumsfeld declared on September 19, 2002, that "no terrorist state poses a greater or more immediate threat to the security of our people that the regime of Saddam Hussein and Iraq." On September 25, 2003, George W. Bush declared that "you can't distinguish between al-Qaeda and Saddam when you talk about the war on terrorism. They're both equally as bad and equally as evil and equally as destructive. . . . The danger is that al-Qaeda becomes an extension of Saddam's madness and his hatred and his capacity to extend weapons of mass destruction around the world." During a closed session in October 2002, the Senate was told that Saddam had chemical and biological weapons that he could launch against the United States by unmanned aerial vehicles from ships in the Atlantic Ocean.[1]

Despite the deafening drumbeat for war within and beyond the White House, the American people remained split. A *New York Times* poll taken in

September 2002 revealed that nearly two-thirds (62 percent) believed that the president should get the approval of Congress for the war, while a third (35 percent) thought that was not necessary. Nearly half (47) percent, believed that the United States should not go to war without first being attacked, while 41 percent supported the country going to war without provocation. Only about a quarter (27 percent) thought the administration had made a convincing case for war, while 64 percent disagreed.[2]

Armed with an advanced word of the polls that backed his arguments, Powell tried to get Bush to recommit to the multilateral policy in a private meeting with him and Rice on September 2. Bush was wishy-washy, saying he supported the idea even though he believed it would fail. Powell sought to rally all the principals during an NSC meeting at Camp David on September 6. Cheney and Rumsfeld led the conservative assault on the realists. Powell managed to buy a little more time to continue his diplomacy at the Security Council and elsewhere. The following day Prime Minister Blair publicly bolstered Powell's position during a joint photo op at Camp David.

During a speech before the UN General Assembly a year and a day after September 11, Bush finally committed himself publicly to seeking a Security Council resolution forcing Iraq either to accept inspections or face war. The deep divisions within the White House between the ideologues and the realists were reflected by the fact that his speech went through twenty-four drafts. After citing the familiar litany of Iraq's crimes against peace and humanity, the president issued a challenge: "All the world now faces a test and the United Nations a difficult and defining moment. Are Security Council resolutions to be honored and enforced or cast aside without consequence? Will the United Nations serve the purpose of its founding or will it be irrelevant?" While Bush did not directly threaten war or Saddam's overthrow, he strongly implied it: "A regime that has lost its legitimacy will also lose its power." In the last draft, the conservatives had deleted the line, "My nation will work with the U.N. Security Council to meet our common challenge." To his credit, Bush recognized the omission and ad-libbed, "We will work with the U.N. Security Council for the necessary resolutions."[3]

The appeal worked. Kofi Annan said he believed "the president's speech galvanized the international community."[4] The secretary-general met with a closed-door caucus of the Arab League on September 14 and implored the twenty-two delegations to pressure Saddam to give in. After Annan left, the league's secretary-general, Amir Moussa, and leader of the foreign ministers, Mahmud Hammud, opened talks with Iraqi foreign minister Naji Sabri.

These talks led to a significant Iraqi concession. In a September 16 letter to Annan, Sabri announced that Iraq would "allow the return of the inspectors without conditions" but then imposed a condition by insisting that any new inspections be tied to ending the sanctions on Iraq. The White House immediately dismissed Iraq's concession as merely an attempt to play for time. On September 21 Baghdad declared that without a trade-off, there would be no inspections.

Two days earlier, on September 19, Bush had sent a formal war resolution to Congress that made as much political as constitutional sense. By making that request two months before the 2002 mid-term elections, the Bush team's timing could not have been better. It would take congressional Democrats five weeks to forge a consensus over how to respond, thus losing valuable time on the campaign trail or on Capitol Hill denouncing the Republicans for wrecking the economy, exploding the national debt, and exacerbating a host of other festering problems. All the war talk likewise distracted most Americans from paying attention to their shrunken incomes, stock portfolios, and retirement accounts.

Tom Daschle and Dick Gephardt, the Democratic Senate and House chiefs, along with nearly all other Democrats, shied away from debating Bush on the merits of war against Iraq. Intimidated by Republican smears that not supporting the war was unpatriotic and even traitorous, most Democrats meekly followed the crowd. At most, a few Democrats raised doubts but did not hold the Bush team's feet to the fire for answers. The only notable cogent argument against the war came from Sen. Robert Byrd of West Virginia, who condemned any unwarranted unilateral aggression as a gross violation of cherished American values.

Although Daschle eventually voted for the war, he at least asked the essential questions: "What new information exists? What threat can be quantified? What has changed in recent months or years? How much will it cost? If we change regimes, who will be in the new regime and has that been thought through?" Although Daschle insisted that he "was more concerned about getting this done right than done quickly," the longer the war issue drowned out all other issues, the worse the Democrats' prospects became in the looming election. When Bush and his team remained mum about the war's justifications, goals, and costs, Daschle shrugged and simply tried to get the issue off the agenda so that his party could get on with the election. But this presented another problem. Daschle was incapable of unifying the Democratic Party on Iraq or any other vital issue.[5]

While the Bush administration stonewalled the release of any important intelligence estimates on Iraq, the British were more forthcoming. Prime Minister Blair presented a case before Parliament on September 24, citing the highlights from a fifty-page intelligence report that claimed that Iraq was hiding chemical and biological weapons and was developing nuclear weapons. The Iraqis could fire missiles with chemical warheads within forty-five minutes of an order to do so. Experts questioned those conclusions. Like the CIA, Parliament's Joint Intelligence Committee concluded that the containment policy was working by "hindering the import of crucial goods for the production of fissible material" and that "while sanctions remain effective Iraq would not be able to produce a nuclear weapon." The prestigious London based International Institute for Strategic Studies echoed that analysis.[6]

Realists continued to press the Bush team to slow the unilateral rush to war. Three of four retired four-star generals who testified before the Senate Armed Forces Committee on September 23, agreed that going it alone against Iraq would be folly. Wesley Clark, John Shalikashvili, and Joseph Hoar all argued that the cost in blood, treasure, rage among Muslims, and global condemnation would not be worth it. Only Thomas McInerney insisted that the United States should conduct war against Iraq in defiance of international law and opinion.

Among the experts, Thomas Friedman typically offered the catchiest retort to the conservative case for war by insisting that while Saddam was homicidal, he was not suicidal.[7] The policy of attack by Bush the son would damage American national security even worse than the pre-Kuwait invasion appeasement policy of Bush the father. It would be the height of folly for George W. Bush to abandon the successful, tough policy of containment and deterrence that his father had eventually initiated and that President Clinton had continued. Deterrence worked. During the Gulf War, Saddam was deterred from using his WMDs by the realization that the United States would retaliate by destroying him and his regime if he did.

President George W. Bush briefly equivocated on the road to war when, on October 1, he admitted that he was open to compromises with Congress and the United Nations over inspections, and that if Saddam did disarm, such an action would constitute "regime change." Was this nuanced remark just a tactic to disarm critics, or did it come from the sudden realization that a war against Iraq might cost a fortune in American blood and treasury? The answer was soon clear.

The fear mongering by conservatives from the White House, Congress, and mass media drowned out the realists and humanitarians, and sharply shifted public opinion. By early October 2002, two-thirds of Americans (67 percent) now backed a war with Iraq, while only 27 percent were opposed. That support, however, fell with a scenario of "substantial American casualties" to 54 percent for and 37 percent against, and "substantial Iraqi civilians casualties" to 49 percent for and 39 percent against. But the biggest drop concerned the United Nations, with 63 percent preferring to wait for the inspections and only 30 percent demanding an immediate war; most Americans favored internationalism over unilateralism. A razor-thin majority still believed in democracy—51 percent—and thought Congress should question Bush more, while only 20 percent thought Congress questioned the president too much. As for Bush's primary goal, 53 percent thought by a two to one margin that this was to remove Saddam as a personal vendetta, and only 29 percent thought it was to remove WMDs. Nonetheless, there was considerable backing for the war as a vendetta.[8]

Bolstered by the polls, Bush took his case to the American people in a televised appearance on October 7, 2002. His speechwriters produced a largely effective political argument, first cataloging Saddam's litany of crimes against peace and humanity, and then presenting "evidence" for hidden WMDs and links between Iraq and Al Qaeda. He ended by demanding that the regime be destroyed before it acquired nuclear weapons. Saddam's evil was vividly expressed: "The dictator of Iraq is a student of Stalin, using murder as a tool of terror and control within his own cabinet, within his own

army, and even within his own family. On Saddam Hussein's orders, opponents have been decapitated, wives and mothers of political opponents have
been systematically raped as a method of intimidation, and political prisoners have been forced to watch their own children being murdered."
Among the more emotionally powerful and intellectually dishonest lines
were: "Confronting the threat posed by Iraq is crucial to winning the war
on terror. . . . We cannot wait for the final proof, the smoking gun, that
could come in the form of a mushroom cloud." In sum, "Saddam Hussein
must disarm himself or, for the sake of peace, we will lead a coalition to disarm him."[9]

CIA Director Tenet offered essentially a rebuttal of Bush's case that same
day. His public admission that Iraq posed "no clear and present danger"
against the United States was a long time coming. All along, the Bush team
had clamped a tight muzzle on Tenet. Frustrated with this obstruction, Bob
Graham, who chaired the Senate Intelligence Committee, had sent on July
22, 2002, the first of several written requests to Tenet for a full disclosure
of the CIA assessment. Three months later, Graham finally got an answer
when Tenet chose to put his duty to his country before the threats that he
might lose his job if he testified.

To the fury of conservatives, Tenet's argument was rooted in a careful
analysis of the evidence rather than in wild assertions that stemmed from
ideological presumptions. Saddam did not and would not for the foreseeable
future have WMDs capable of striking the United States. Even if he had
them, he would be deterred from using them for fear of massive retaliation.
The only plausible scenario for Saddam to order the launch of chemical and
biological weapons against the United States would be if Washington ordered the invasion of Iraq. Likewise he would only consider giving WMDs
to terrorists if faced with the destruction of his regime. America's containment policy toward Iraq had been highly successful in thwarting his impe-
rialist dreams, despite a certain amount of smuggling and hidden weapon
programs. As for Iraq's ties with Al Qaeda, there may have been sporadic
contacts, but there was no evidence that Baghdad was aware of, let alone
aided in, September 11.[10]

Essentially the CIA director diplomatically explained that the conservatives had twisted everything inside out. The containment policy would deter

Saddam from ever considering, let alone launching, WMDs against the United States, in the extremely unlikely scenario that he acquired the capacity to deliver such an attack on the other side of the world. But if he actually did have WMDs, he would not hesitate to use them against any invader. Thus, ironically, Bush's policy of war against Iraq could provoke the very attack that the president and his fellow conservatives claimed that they wanted to prevent.

Yet the assertions of the conservatives and fears of most Americans prevailed over the careful analyses of the realists. On October 11, 2002, Congress overwhelmingly voted to grant Bush a blank check to wage war against Iraq. The final tally in the House was 296 to 133, with 126 Democrats, 6 Republicans, and 1 independent opposed. In the Senate the vote went 78 to 22, with 21 Democrats and 1 independent opposed. Congress resolved that "the president is authorized to use the armed forces of the United States as he determines to be necessary and appropriate to: defend the national security of the United States against the continuing threat posed by Iraq; and enforce all relevant United Nations Security Council resolutions regarding Iraq." The only requirement was that the president explain to the House speaker and Senate president pro tempore within forty-eight hours of an attack why he did so.[11]

Congress had not granted a president such stunning leeway to wage war as he wished on such utterly contrived notions since 1964, when with near unanimity it approved President Lyndon Johnson's Gulf of Tonkin Resolution for Vietnam. Indeed the excuses for war that both presidents Johnson and Bush paraded were as disingenuous as the congressional support for those wars was shrilly enthusiastic.

5

The Inspections

Unlike Congress, the UN Security Council was no pushover for war. The
Bush administration's initial draft Security Council resolution combined bellicose demands for inspections and for war if Iraq failed to comply. The reaction was almost uniformly negative. Presidents Jacques Chirac, Vladimir
Putin, and Jiang Zemin, the respective heads of France, Russia, and China,
all expressed skepticism over Iraqi weapons capacity and other Bush claims,
and condemned any unilateral American war against Iraq as a gross violation
of international law. Yet each leader was open to compromise. Jiang was the
first to indicate that he would not oppose a resolution as long as it did not
give an automatic green light to an invasion. Chirac proposed a two-step
resolution process, with the first demanding inspections but shorn of any
belligerent talk. Any refusal by Saddam to comply would be countered with
a second resolution authorizing force.

Conservatives predictably condemned and spurned these sensible compromises. The result was deadlock. Of the four other states with veto power,
Britain backed the United States, China sat the fence, and France and Russia
were opposed. And then there were the ten nonpermanent members to convince—Mexico, Syria, Colombia, Ireland, Norway, Singapore, Bulgaria,
Cameroon, Mauritius, and Guinea—each with its own interests and arguments to promote.

Powell and Blair kept up the pressure on Bush and the other ideologues
that if they did not give some ground, the resolution would die. Bush signaled

that war was not inevitable when, on October 27, he repeated his expansive definition of regime change: "If [Saddam] were to meet all the conditions of the United Nations, the conditions that I've described very clearly in terms that everybody can understand, that in itself will signal that the regime has changed." In other words Saddam could stay in power if he complied with the Security Council resolutions. Then, on October 23, Ambassador Negroponte presented a resolution that authorized the use of force against Iraq if it were found in "material breach" of previous Security Council resolutions.

Those concessions were enough for the White House to entice each reluctant Security Council member one by one. On November 8 the Security Council voted unanimously, 15 to zero, for Resolution 1441. The biggest surprise was Syria, which justified its vote with the claim that the resolution would actually prevent a war against Iraq.

Resolution 1441 empowered the inspection teams at any time to interview anyone or inspect anywhere and imposed a series of deadlines for Iraq's compliance, the violation of any one of which would be considered a material breach and thus legal grounds for war. Within a week, by November 15, Saddam had to acknowledge whether he would accept the resolution. If he did so the two inspection heads and their teams, Hans Blix for chemical and biological weapons and Mohamed ElBaradei for nuclear weapons, would arrive in Baghdad on November 18 to set up operations. Spot inspections would begin as early as November 25. By December 8 Saddam was to submit a list of all his programs, facilities, and actual weapons. A full report of the two inspection teams would be submitted to the Security Council no later than February 21, 2003.

The UN inspection teams were empowered to reveal whether the conservative claims about Iraqi WMDs were true or mere delusions. During nearly two months in Iraq, the two teams, whose combined personnel numbered more than 250, made at least 780 visits to over 350 sites. ElBaradei and Blix delivered their respective preliminary reports on January 27, 2003. Neither found any evidence of significant Iraqi violations of the array of UN Security Council resolutions on WMDs. Both asked for more time to complete their work. ElBaradei's report stated that Iraq's nuclear program appeared to have been completely dismantled: "We have to date no evidence that Iraq has revived its nuclear weapons program since the elimination of the program in the 1990s." Blix's conclusions were more ambiguous and complex. While he lauded Iraq's efforts as "a very significant piece of real disarmament" and cooperation on procedural issues, the central question still begged to be answered: what had happened to all the chemical and biological weapons that Saddam was known to have amassed? The Iraqis claimed that they had destroyed those weapons but offered no proof that they had done so. The records, they claimed, were missing.[1]

Saddam's arsenal of chemical weapons was the best known. Baghdad admitted that it once had had 11,131 chemical weapons and warheads, 105 tons of stockpiled sarin, tabun, and mustard agents, and 553 pieces of chemical weapons production equipment at fifteen facilities, but had no documents to account for 550 R-400 missiles (SS-23s), including 157 with biological agents. In all, the inspectors could account for the whereabouts of only two thousand shells or bombs and warheads capable of carrying chemical or biological agents. So where were the rest, and were their warheads all empty? Only Saddam and his closest officials knew for sure.[2]

As for biological weapons, Saddam had denied any development until Hussein Kamal, the dictator's son-in-law, defected in 1995. The Iraqis admitted that they once had 22,000 gallons of anthrax and 100,000 gallons of botulinum toxin but claimed that they had destroyed it all. Here again the inspectors could not verify the claim. Other reports indicated that the Iraqis had amassed 12,500 gallons of anthrax, 2,500 gallons of gas gangrene (clostridium perfringens), 1,250 gallons of alflatoxin, and 2,000 of botulinum. If those weapons still existed, how deadly were they? Any botulinum toxin made before 1990 would now be harmless, but the other agents could still be viable if they were properly stored. The inspectors concluded that by the Gulf War's end, the Iraqis had two dozen Scud missiles and 550 R-400s, of which 160 were adapted for delivering chemical or biological agents. While that sounded formidable enough, the effectiveness of those weapons was questionable. By detonating on impact, these bombs and missiles most likely would have incinerated most and perhaps all of their deadly agents.[3]

The reactions of the realists and ideologues to the reimposition of inspections and the subsequent reports were diametrically opposed. The realists rejoiced. The Bush team's military buildup and bluster had won. Saddam was more boxed in and diminished than ever. Even though no WMDs had been found, Iraq was being systematically laid bare in an unprecedented intelligence windfall. The Security Council resolution, Saddam's concessions, and the sweeping inspections made an American war against Iraq practically unnecessary and morally reprehensible. For conservatives the inspections and reports were ideological disasters. They faced a worsening crisis as Saddam complied with one demand after another, and the inspectors found Iraq apparently denuded of any WMDs. How then could a war be justified?

The conservative solution to this conundrum was simply to denounce the inspections and assert more onerous and humiliating demands on Saddam until he finally stopped conceding. The fact that Iraq posed absolutely no present or conceivable future threat to its neighbors, let alone the United States, was irrelevant. The conservatives were determined to destroy Saddam's regime even if Iraq was decisively disarmed and contained. Conservatives in the administration, Congress, and mass media began pillorying the inspectors as all but Saddam's collaborators and agents.

The credibility of the reports obviously rested on the independence of the two inspection teams. While both ElBaradei and Blix defended themselves against the slanderous onslaught, Blix was more outspoken, insisting that "I did not tailor my report to the political wishes or hopes in Baghdad or Washington or any other place."[4] Of course, for conservatives that very refusal to be the Bush team's puppet was the source of his treachery. Blix criticized those in the White House and beyond who distorted his report's findings. The inspectors found no evidence to back the conservative claims that the Iraqis were hiding and moving illicit materials or scientists around Iraq or even outside the country, nor did they find any links between Iraq and September 11. He denied the allegation that Iraqi agents had penetrated the inspection teams. Finally he dismissed the administration's claim that only war would resolve the lingering questions about the missing materials. The inspections were successful and would completely disarm Iraq if they were given enough time.

The conservatives upped the ante with yet another demand: Saddam must go. Disarmament now took second place to regime change. Conservatives wanted to boast that Bush had finished the job his father had begun. The president himself said on January 30 that he would welcome exile for Saddam and his inner circle. Rumsfeld went so far as to hint that a departure might be appeased with a grant of immunity.

Realists pointed out the illogic in this latest twist in the Bush team's policy. If hidden WMDs were the key problem, then Saddam's exile would most likely do nothing to reveal and eliminate them. If the weapons actually did exist, only inspections or war had a chance of rooting them out. Any successor was likely to be just as ruthless and anti-American as Saddam, if perhaps more subtle. But the intelligence community agreed that Saddam had no intention of retiring to, say, Libya, and living quietly off the several billion dollars he had looted from Iraq. Saddam was convinced that he would either crush any American invasion or die gloriously, fighting in the rubble. Regardless, he hoped to be remembered for eternity as a great Arab leader.

So how serious was Bush's call for exile? That option mollified those who feared that administration was hell-bent for war. Other governments, including Saudi Arabia, quietly backed the idea. But when Saddam inevitably spurned the invitation, it gave the Bush administration the excuse for war.[5]

Until late January the resistance of realists within and beyond the White House had slowed the conservative march toward war against Iraq. Then, on January 13, 2003, Bush summoned Powell to the Oval Office and told him he had made the final decision for war. The secretary of state tried to open the president's mind to the Pandora's box he was dead set on yanking open. "You know the consequences. You know you're going to be owning this place? You are going to be the proud owner of 25 million people. You will own all their hopes, aspirations, and problems. You'll own it all." And the cost would be crushing. "You own it, you fix it."[6]

But even as Powell fruitlessly tried to get Bush to understand the financial, political, legal, and moral implications of his decision, he was shifting from the containment to the conquest camp. His turning point came during a Security Council meeting on January 20. The topic was supposed to be terrorism, but French foreign minister Dominique de Villepin used it to demand more time for the inspections and to voice his opposition to any war against Iraq.

While Powell was publicly unflappable, he was privately seething at what he felt was Villepin's grandstanding. In other words France should not support more inspections without the threat of war if Iraq failed to comply.

Villepin agreed. In a classic example of "mirror image," the French and others felt that it was the Bush administration that had betrayed their trust by never intending to allow the inspections a chance to work, but instead intended to use Resolution 1441 as an excuse for war even if there were no weapons and the Iraqis cooperated.

In that, Powell insisted on his own sincerity; as for the conservatives, they could speak for themselves. The secretary of state now agreed that it was time to give war a chance. Ironically, Powell was throwing in the realist towel just as the inspectors were revealing that the Bush administration's allegations against Iraq were nothing but utter delusions.[7]

6

The Second Resolution

Should unproven allegations be the basis for the unilateral American invasion of Iraq and destruction of Saddam's regime? The Bush team vehemently asserted that they could, should, and would. But two powerful voices—British Prime Minister Tony Blair and Secretary of State Colin Powell—countered that without Security Council approval, the Bush administration's war against Iraq would not only be illegal, but also prohibitively costly in American treasure, blood, and honor. Bush and his conservative advisers grudgingly agreed to seek a UN Security Council resolution authorizing the war.

Achieving that resolution would have been an uphill battle even under the best of diplomatic circumstances. The United States needed nine of the fifteen votes and no veto by a permanent member. Only two countries openly supported the war—Britain and Bulgaria; France, China, Syria, and Russia were openly opposed. To win, Bush needed six of the swing votes of Guinea, Cameroon, Columbia, Mauritius, Singapore, Norway, Ireland, and Mexico. Even if the resolution got nine votes, it faced a possible veto by the opposed permanent members, France, Russia, and China. The odds of passage were long indeed.

Over the previous two years, the Bush administration's bellicose actions and attitudes had repeatedly offended, in varying degrees, every Security Council member, including those who supported a war against Iraq. The vitriolic conservative contempt for multilateral diplomacy and the glee with which it rejected treaties on such issues as global warming, the nuclear weapons test ban, and the International Criminal Court came back to haunt them. The most important reason for opposition to the war against Iraq, however, was the lack of any solid evidence to substantiate the Bush administration's charges.

As if all that were not crippling enough, the Bush team took a feeble diplomatic hand and weakened it. They prevented their best asset, Colin Powell, from conducting the sort of shuttle diplomacy that might have swung a crucial vote or two. Instead, the conservatives played hardball with the undecided countries, hinting darkly that any that did not vote with the United States would suffer economic reprisals. This was a genuine threat against the poorer countries and largely a bluff against the more powerful, such as Germany and France. The American and European economies are so entwined that any retaliation would likely have hurt the United States as well. But the Bush team had a much more painless way to retaliate against two of the Security Council members. They made it especially clear to Russia and France that their extensive business contracts with Iraq might well be voided by the post-Saddam regime that the United States set up, while Iraq's repayment of debts to those countries would be postponed or canceled altogether as other needs took priority. But all the conservative chest-thumping, table-pounding, arm-twisting, and grandstanding, which most Americans found so convincing, alienated the dignified Europeans, Africans, Asians, and Latin Americans on the Security Council and beyond.[1]

The climax came on February 5, 2003, when Powell, with CIA chief Tenet sitting pointedly behind him, presented the conservative case for war before the Security Council. Powell put the best spin on what was at most circumstantial evidence. He presented a pile of telephone intercepts, satellite photos, and eyewitness accounts, all linked with conjecture, to argue that Saddam was hiding vast stockpiles of WMDs and sponsoring terrorism. He raised important questions about the fate of missing chemical and biological weapons that Iraq was known to have produced—a thousand tons of chemical agents, from one hundred to five hundred tons of nerve agents, and at least seven mobile biological laboratories packed with the world's deadliest germs. He insisted that a top Al Qaeda operative, Abu Musaab al-Zarqawi, who had operated a terrorist group in the Kurdish region of Iraq for the past eight months and was said to have been responsible for the murder of

Laurence Foley, an American diplomat in Jordan, could not have done so without Baghdad's support. But Powell revealed no concrete proof that Saddam had either hidden weapons or links with Al Qaeda. To his credit, Powell deleted the yellowcake and centrifuge lies from his speech. Yet, he repeated other myths, most notoriously that "a sinister nexus" existed "between Iraq and the Al Qaeda terrorist network, a nexus that combines classic terrorist organizations and modern methods of murder."[2] The presentation wooed no Security Council converts.

A couple of weeks later those opposed to the war found more evidence that the disarmament regime was working. On February 22 Hans Blix declared that Iraq's Al-Samoud 2 missiles violated the 1991 cease-fire agreement under Security Council Resolution 687 since they had a range of more than 150 kilometers, and he ordered the arsenal destroyed. The Iraqis protested that the range was within the limits once the guidance system was installed in the missile. But when Blix insisted, the Iraqis began to comply by dismantling the 120 missiles, along with all the components and equipment used to make them. This was an enormous concession in the face of an all but inevitable American invasion. These missiles had the potential to inflict serious casualties on the attackers.

French president Chirac had led the antiwar resistance, declaring that he would not just vote against, but veto any resolution authorizing war against Iraq. Though Chirac and Bush took diametrically opposed positions, they did so for the same reasons: each not only thought he was right, but because his position was overwhelmingly popular at home. On March 6 France, Russia, and Germany jointly declared that they "will not allow" passage of a resolution authorizing war against Iraq. Instead they circulated a draft proposal to give the inspectors another four months. The Bush administration angrily blocked it.

Prime Minister Blair once again tried to bridge the daunting gap between the Bush administration and most of the rest of the world. On March 12 he proposed six conditions for peace that he hoped would sway the Security Council holdouts. Saddam had to appear on television, admit in Arabic that he had been cheating, and promise to disarm. At least thirty of Iraq's leading scientists and their families would be airlifted to Cyprus for debriefing. Iraq had either to produce all its remaining chemical and biological weapons or prove that they had been destroyed. But these proposals went nowhere. The White House gave them only lukewarm support, while most other Security Council members coldly dismissed them.

Bush and Blair said they would have been satisfied with a "moral victory" in which they got nine votes required for passage that would have been vetoed by France. But after weeks of effort, Powell and Blair could not squeeze the votes out of a majority, let alone nine members. Faced with this humiliating defeat, they chose to withdraw the resolution without a formal vote.

The Bush administration would go to war against Iraq without the UN Security Council's approval—indeed in defiance of its overwhelming disapproval. On every practical, legal, and moral level, the Iraq War would be a dream come true for America's enemies, Muslim and non-Muslim alike. Perhaps the most vital force multiplier for terrorists is to goad their enemy into overreacting to a perceived threat with massive assaults on suspected terrorist strongholds. The resulting collateral damage and death in turn alienates fence-sitters to join the terrorist cause. Ironically, it was not terrorists but conservatives who goaded America to war against Iraq.

7

The Search for Allies

In the months leading up to the invasion, as the Bush administration appeared determined to go to war against Iraq, American realists and humanitarians, as well as ever more governments and peoples around the world, became increasingly concerned. Opposition naturally erupted among America's long-standing enemies and rivals. But even America's allies and friends split bitterly between those who opposed and those who supported the rush to war.

Most European governments seemed at first to unite against the march to war. Chris Patten, the European Union's foreign affairs chief, cautioned the Bush administration against an arrogant hubris and a militant unilateralism: "The stunning and unexpectedly rapid success of the military campaign in Afghanistan was a tribute to American capacity. But it has perhaps reinforced some dangerous instincts: that the projection of military power is the only basis of true security; that the U.S. can rely on no one but itself; and that allies may be useful as an optional extra. . . . The lesson of September 11 is that we need both American leadership and international cooperation on an unprecedented scale. The unilateralist urge is not wicked. Simply it is ultimately ineffective and self-defeating."[1]

Within the European Union, French president Jacques Chirac and German Chancellor Gerhard Schroeder were the most outspoken against an Iraq war. Schroeder offered the sensible advice that the Bush administration not advocate such a undertaking "without thinking of the political consequences and without having a political concept for the entire Middle East."[2] But the French and Germans overplayed their hand with a claim that they spoke for all European governments.

Dissent eventually belied that conceit. In early 2003 the Bush team's stance was bolstered by two open letters of support endorsed by eighteen European prime ministers. The first letter of January 30, was signed by Britain, the Czech Republic, Denmark, Hungary, Italy, Poland, Portugal, and Spain. This was followed on February 6 by another letter issued by thirteen governments including nine from eastern Europe, specifically Estonia, Latvia, Lithuania, Slovakia, Albania, Croatia, Bulgaria, Romania, and Macedonia. The latter was especially thought provoking; until recently the peoples of all those countries had suffered exploitation from brutal communist dictatorships. All of these prime ministers faced the threat of losing the next election, since public opinion in nearly all of those countries overwhelmingly opposed the conservative crusade.[3]

The letters enraged President Chirac who warned that the signatories were "reckless of the danger in aligning themselves too rapidly with the American position." He threatened to boycott the pending membership of the eastern European states in the European Union, which was scheduled for May 1, 2004. But Chirac's effort backfired.[4]

The conflicts over war or peace with Iraq spread to NATO. A bitter deadlock emerged after Ankara asked NATO to reposition Patriot missiles, AWACS surveillance planes, and other equipment to protect Turkey from a possible Iraqi retaliatory attack if a war erupted. NATO requires unanimity before any redeployment among its members can take place. Although sixteen members approved, Germany, France, and Belgium blocked the proposal, arguing that to go along would tacitly back an Iraq war.

The Americans were justifiably irritated with the impasse. After all, the White House had originally agreed to go through NATO for those transfers when some members complained that the organization was being ignored. As Nicholas Burns, America's ambassador to NATO, put it: "We really want the alliance to be with us in this crisis with Iraq, and we think it is a test of the alliance's credibility to meet Turkey's request for its allies' help."[5] The impasse lasted three weeks before the United States used a procedural device to bypass the resistance and gain approval for the transfer. But the bitterness lingered long after.

In the end, although most European governments supported the invasion, only Britain and Poland initially supplied troops. This was an especially courageous decision by Prime Minister Blair, since a survey revealed that only 13 percent of Britons backed their country joining the United States in warring against Iraq without a Security Council resolution. That figure, however, jumped to 53 percent with Security Council approval. Blair could have used that overwhelming opposition as an excuse to back out of the war. But the prime minister stood by his commitment despite the potentially heavy political and moral costs to him and his party, which might eventually have to be paid.[6]

Like Europe, the Middle East at first appeared united against the war but split as the Bush team pressured its traditional allies in the region for help. Most Middle East regimes at once despised and supported Saddam Hussein. Not only was the dictator a fellow Arab and Muslim, but his police state held together a mosaic of contentious ethnic, religious, tribal, and economic groups. Should Saddam fall, the country could dissolve into anarchy and splinter among the Kurds in the north and Shiites in the south, leaving a rump Sunni state in the center. Only Shiite Iran would rejoice in an autonomous or outright independent oil-rich Shiite realm sitting on the Persian Gulf. Nearly every Arab state had a Sunni government and feared the spread of Iranian and Shiite influence across the region.

With its own rebellious Kurdish region, Turkey opposed an autonomous or independent Kurdistan in northern Iraq. All the countries surrounding Iraq dreaded the cutoff of trade and the flood of refugees that a war would provoke. Prince Saud al-Faisal, the Saudi foreign minister, spoke for virtually everyone when he disparaged the idea that the Americans would bring peace, prosperity, and democracy to a postwar Iraq. "If you get chaos," he argued, "how will democracy flower in Iraq?"[7]

The reasoned arguments of regional allies against the war were drowned out by emotional protests in mosques and streets across the Muslim world. The Al-Azhar Mosque and University in Cairo is about the closest Sunni Muslims have to a Vatican. The clerics and their fatwas, or legal rulings, are the most respected among Sunnis. After the American invasion, Al-Azhar's Islamic Research Center would call for a jihad against the United States and its allies for their Iraq crusade. Those calls were echoed by other prominent clerics across the Sunni world.

Regional allies were vital to the Pentagon's plan. Although heavy bombers flying from the island of Diego Garcia in the Indian Ocean and fighter bombers and cruise missiles launched from the fleet within the Persian Gulf would devastate Iraq, that formidable firepower alone might not be enough for victory. Bases in the region would be important for additional bombers and ground troops that would make a certain victory swifter and easier.

America's allies Turkey, Jordan, Saudi Arabia, and Egypt repeatedly warned that any war could destabilize the entire region politically and economically. They pleaded with Bush to continue the successful containment and deterrence policy that stifled Saddam's ambitions while slowly eroding his regime. They officially refused to aid Bush's war against Iraq unless the Security Council authorized it.

Yet beneath the antiwar rhetoric, several Arab states provided varying types of help to the United States. Kuwait was the launching pad for the ground offensive into Iraq, while the regional headquarters for the invasion was located in Qatar. Saudi Arabia denied that the United States was conducting its air war from Prince Sultan Air Base on its territory even though it was. Jordan allowed several hundred American troops on its soil to man and guard Patriot missile batteries.[8]

The friendly Arab governments tried to resolve the crisis with diplomacy. In March 2003 two meetings of the twenty-two-member Arab League failed to reach a consensus. A majority rejected a call by the United Arab Emirates for Saddam to step down. Likewise, an emergency meeting of the fifty-seven-member Organization of the Islamic Conference in March was nearly as acrimonious and deadlocked. On the war's eve a delegation of foreign ministers from Tunisia, Lebanon, and Bahrain prepared to fly to Baghdad and convince Saddam to go into exile. That delegation never got off the ground when the Iraqi dictator rejected the mission.[9]

The dissident country most damaging to the Bush administration's war plans was Turkey. The White House wanted to open a second front against Iraq, with 62,000 troops led by the Fourth Infantry Division invading from southern Turkey. The Turks, however, saw no good and much evil in the conservative crusade, including a tidal wave of refugees, economic depression, and eventually a Kurdish free state on its border, which in turn would inspire a renewed liberation struggle among the Kurds in Turkey itself.

Moreover, a Pew Research Center survey found that 83 percent of Turks opposed allowing the Americans to use their homeland to attack Iraq. To support Bush's war would be both an economic disaster for Turkey and a political disaster for its ruling party. Ankara thus tried to sidestep the Bush team's demands. The Turks argued that any question of war be deferred until the inspections were completed. Turkey would not participate in a war unauthorized by the Security Council.

But the Bush administration refused to take no for an answer and upped the pressure by dangling the prospect of massive economic aid in return for the alliance. Much against its will, Ankara found itself in embarrassingly public negotiations with the White House over the price of its alliance. In early January, Marc Grossman, the under secretary of state for policy, flew to Ankara with a $14 billion deal, including a $4 billion grant to guarantee a $10 billion loan. Abdullah Gül and Recip Tayyip Erdoğan, the respective sitting and pending prime ministers, immediately rejected the offer as inadequate. This began what would become two months of haggling. The final American offer was $6 billion in direct grants, which would be used as a guarantee for up to $24 billion in loans. The Turks demanded $10 billion in grants and $22 billion in loans.

Meanwhile Gül did make some concessions. He and his parliamentary majority went along with a Washington request to upgrade the bases that might be used by American troops. He then agreed to ask parliament on February 18 to permit the American military to attack Iraq from Turkey. The parliamentary debate lasted ten days. Although Gül's Justice Development Party enjoyed a parliamentary majority, the measure failed to pass on March 1.

The negotiations between America and Turkey did not end there. Ironically the United States had to contain Turkey's ambitions to seize northern Iraq with its oil fields and its Kurdish population. Iraq's Kurds had enjoyed autonomy since the Gulf War, and their fear was that Turkey might use the war as a pretext to conquer them. In a February 13 letter to Bush, Massoud Barzani and Jalal Talabani, the respective leaders of the Kurdistan Democratic Party and the Patriotic Union of Kurdistan, expressed their fears that "Turkey's real agenda is to crush our experiment in democratic self-government," and they called for American protection against that threat. The Iraqi Kurds boasted of having 80,000 militiamen ready to ally with the United States, although after the war began only several hundred actually showed up to assist operations. The White House eventually elicited a pledge from Ankara not to invade and occupy northern Iraq.[10]

For years Washington had endured the Sisyphean challenge of trying to forge unity among Iraq's opposition groups into an effective political and military alliance. The three broad divisions of Kurd, Sunni, and Shiite are in turn split among 150 tribes and 2,000 smaller clans.

The largest opposition group was the previously mentioned Iraqi National Congress, founded in 1992 and led by the Shiite Ahmed Chalabi. The Iraq Liberation Act of 1998 embraced the INC as the spearhead of opposition to Saddam. The CIA and State Department, however, questioned whether that endorsement may have been misplaced in an INC characterized as inept, splintered, profligate, and corrupt. White House conservatives led by Cheney, Rumsfeld, Wolfowitz, and Wayne Downing, the deputy national security adviser for combating terrorism, angrily dismissed such skepticism and vociferously championed the INC. Yet, CIA and State Department skepticism was well founded. Half a year after Saddam was toppled even the Defense Intelligence Agency (DIA) would admit that two-thirds of the "intelligence" provided by Chalabi's agents before the war was completely wrong, while less than a third had any potential value. The CIA had warned that these defectors had lied or exaggerated their importance just to get better deals, but the DIA allowed itself to be suckered, with disastrous consequences for American national security.[11]

Chalabi failed to transform the INC from an umbrella group into a more cohesive organization during a congress held in mid-December 2002 in London. After days of wrangling, the 330 delegates from six major groups and a score of smaller ones forged a consensus on two principles. One was to bar American dominance of their group or country. The other was to create a federal parliamentary system for postwar Iraq. But they deadlocked on all other issues.[12]

Critics argued that the INC's divisiveness lay with Chalabi himself, whom they dismissed as bungling and corrupt. Indeed, decades earlier Chalabi had fled Jordan after absconding with more than a million dollars he received in an elaborate fraud scheme that led to the currency's collapse. Many feared that his greed and incompetence would be disastrous for Iraq if he were ever allowed to participate in governing that benighted country. Those fears would be realized.

Alternatives to the INC were even more discouraging. Although the White House would eventually tap the CIA and State Department favorite, Ayad Allawi, to serve as interim prime minister, his Iraqi National Accord, founded in 1990, was largely a paper organization with a phantom army. The London-based Constitutional Monarchy Movement led by Sharif Ali bin al-Hussein had existed since the king's murder in 1958 but had no significant following. The only exile group with genuine political cohesion and military power was the absolute worst choice from Washington's point of view. The Supreme Council for Islamic Revolution in Iraq, founded in 1982 and led by Muhammad Bakr al-Hakim, numbered about eight thousand fighters and was based in Tehran.

The Kurds were just as bitterly divided as the Arabs. Massoud Barzani, whose Kurdistan Democratic Party had been founded in 1946 and numbered from fifteen thousand to twenty-five thousand armed men, had a hatred for rival Kurdish leaders that exceeded his hatred for Saddam. He actually encouraged Baghdad to attack Talabani's Patriotic Union of Kurdistan, which had been founded in 1974 and numbered about fifteen thousand fighters.

These were just the most prominent Iraqi opposition groups. There were dozens more, each with highly ambitious, grossly exaggerated numbers of warriors and no real prospects for seizing power. The White House failed repeatedly to forge unity among the rivals, as one or more groups would denounce and boycott scheduled conferences. These were the people whom the Bush administration would champion as the legitimate rulers of a liberated Iraq.

8

Cheerleaders and Dissidents

The conservatives proved to be extremely adept in at least one political skill: rallying most Americans to the Iraq War and shouting down any dissent. Their most effective means of doing so was by co-opting the mainstream media behind the conservative crusade.[1] During the buildup to the war, the Bush administration, and its allies in Congress and the conservative media, accused any analysts, editors, or institutions with realist or humanitarian objections to war against Iraq of being unpatriotic or outright treasonous. This intimidated all but the most courageous opponents to the war.

As usual, most Americans confused patriotism with unconditional support for the president's policies. And they enthusiastically gave it. The Bush team's ability to market its war through the mass media powerfully shaped public opinion. A *New York Times*/CBS survey in mid-February 2003 found that support for a war against Iraq had soared to 53 percent from 28 percent in just a month. Thanks to the conservative power to spin the mass media, and contrary to all evidence, an astonishing 42 percent of Americans believed that Saddam was behind September 11, while 55 percent believed he was allied with Al Qaeda, up from only 3 percent immediately after the attack. Yet support for the war had some soft spots. Only 37 percent supported an immediate war, while 59 percent wanted to give the inspections more time, and 63 percent thought that the United States should only fight with allies. These figures would shift dramatically once the bombs started dropping, to three-quarters supporting the war and believing that Saddam was responsible for September 11.[2]

Conservatives within and beyond the White House mercilessly assailed any dissidents. Typical was the fate of Tom Daschle, the Senate minority leader and a Vietnam War veteran, who pointed out on March 17, 2003, that the pending war reflected a failure of diplomacy. That simple truism triggered a vitriolic attack by conservatives within and beyond the White House that smeared Daschle as unpatriotic. Thereafter Daschle and nearly all other Democrats uttered nothing but patriotic platitudes regarding the war. Sen. John Kerry, another Vietnam veteran, was among the few who dared to stand up to the conservative bullying. "I say to the president," he boldly stated, "show respect for the process of international diplomacy because it is not only right, it can make America stronger. Mr. President, do not rush to war."[3]

Humanitarian politicians were easy targets for the conservatives whose McCarthyite tirades deeply troubled thoughtful Americans. Yet even the average naive, ignorant, fearful citizen might pause for thought when the target of conservative vitriol was a general with a chest full of medals. Retired generals Norman Schwarzkopf, Anthony Zinni, and Wesley Clark all opposed the Iraq War. Schwarzkopf called for giving the inspectors more time and resources to do the job. Zinni wondered "which planet" the conservatives "live on because it isn't the one that I travel." He argued that "to solve this through violent action, we're on the wrong course. First of all, I don't see that it's necessary. Second of all I think that war and violence are a very last resort."[4]

The one of four Americans who were Catholic faced a tough choice between the conflicting demands of their president and their pope. Pope John Paul II repeatedly spoke out against the war, calling it "a defeat for humanity" and ending a sermon with a resounding "No to war!" America's Catholic bishops echoed the pontiff's message. Although they condemned Saddam's brutal regime, they declared on November 13, 2002, that there was no justification for war against Iraq. Indeed, they argued that an American invasion would cause more evil than it could conceivably mitigate even if Bush's accusations and promises were true.[5]

America's leading scientists also publicly opposed the war. The day after Hans Blix issued his inspection report, forty-one American Nobel Prize winners in science and economics issued a declaration opposing "a preventive war against Iraqi without broad international support. Military operations against Iraq may indeed lead to a relatively swift victory in the short term. But war is characterized by surprise, human loss, and unintended consequences. Even with a victory we believe that the medical, economic, environmental, moral, spiritual, political, and legal consequences of an American preventive attack on Iraq would undermine, not protect, U.S. security and standing in the world."[6] That statement was prescient on all counts.

The AFL-CIO executive committee broke with its tradition of silence on foreign policy issues and unanimously approved a resolution criticizing Bush's war. They argued, "The president has not fulfilled his responsibility to make a compelling and coherent explanation to the American people and the world as to the need for military action against Iraq at this time."[7]

One career diplomat resigned to protest the Bush team's pending Iraq invasion. John Brady Kiesling, the political counselor at the embassy in Athens, stated in his resignation letter, "Our fervent pursuit of war with Iraq is driving us to squander the international legitimacy that has been America's most potent weapon of both offense and defense since the days of Woodrow Wilson. . . . We should ask ourselves why we have failed to persuade more of the world that a war with Iraq is necessary. We have over the past two years done too much to assert to our world partners that narrow and mercenary U.S. interests override the cherished values of our partners."[8]

Those who opposed the war would have been powerfully boosted had it been publicly revealed that in the month before the invasion, Saddam had offered stunning concessions. Former Iraqi intelligence chief Tahir Jalil Habbush met with a Lebanese American businessman, Imad Hage, who in turn eventually conveyed this message to the White House. Saddam Hussein would let American inspectors and troops search for the alleged WMDs, he would turn over a suspect in the 1993 World Trade Center attacks, cooperate with America's war on terrorism, openly support the White House's position on the Israeli-Palestinian conflict, hold national elections overseen by the United Nations, and give American firms lucrative business contracts in Iraq.[9] How different America and the world would have been had the Bush administration not rejected these sweeping concessions.

The case for war against Iraq was simple according to the ideologues but simple-minded according to the realists. In violation of Security Council resolutions, Iraq had cached biological and chemical weapons, was developing nuclear weapons, was involved in the September 11 attacks, and sooner or later would strike America with WMDs. The policies of containment and deterrence against Iraq had failed. The only alternative was a war that would destroy Saddam Hussein's dictatorship and its WMDs, and remake Iraq as a model of democracy, prosperity, and peace for the Middle East and the world.

Humanitarians and realists both opposed the war for the same spectrum of reasons but emphasized different aspects of that spectrum. Humanitarians argued against the war primarily because it would leave the Iraqi people worse off; realists opposed the war because it would leave America worse off. The humanitarian position was straightforward enough and has been easily proven by the hard statistics of death, destruction, refugees, and impoverishment that Iraqis have suffered since the war began. The realist argument was more complex.[10]

From a realist perspective, not only did Iraq pose no threat to the United States, it was actually a key component of American security in the Persian Gulf region. From August 1990 to March 2003, Washington and the UN Security Council pursued a triple containment policy in the Persian Gulf. The economic sanctions and weapon inspections atop the destruction during the Gulf War depleted and contained Iraq's potential for aggression. Yet Washington left Saddam Hussein in Baghdad with enough military power to brutally suppress Islamism within Iraq and deter any attack by Iran. That triple containment strategy was an enormous success at a miniscule cost to American taxpayer and none for American blood.

Realists contemptuously dismissed conservative claims of an alliance between Saddam and bin Laden, and an imminent Iraqi threat to attack the United States with WMDs. They pointed out that Saddam and bin Laden were actually ideological enemies who wished destruction on each other. As for WMDs, realists assumed that Saddam might well have squirreled away some chemical and biological weapons, but most likely they were not operational and most certainly they would only be used to deter or, if that failed, counterattack an invasion. Iraqi launch vehicles could have carried chemical or biological warheads at most only a few hundred miles, about seven thousand miles short of hitting America's eastern seaboard. Saddam may have been a brutal dictator responsible for nearly a million unnecessary deaths, but he was not suicidal. He may have occasionally rattled the bars of his containment cage, but he did not dare try to break out. He lacked both the capacity and intent to do so, and knew all too well that that aggression would trigger his destruction.

The economic sanctions had devastated Iraq's economy. Iraq sold virtually no oil from 1990 to 1997. These lost revenues may have been as much as $250 billion. After the oil-for-food program began in 1997, Saddam and his henchmen managed to siphon off about $10.1 billion, or 15 percent of the money Iraq earned from oil sales through 2002. That money was mostly used to boost the bank accounts of the elite, not the prowess of Iraq's military. During the 1990s Iraq's military budget was only about $1.5 billion a year, down from $47 billion at the time of the Gulf War![11]

Brent Scowcroft, the national security adviser for George H. W. Bush, clearly warned of the dire consequences for American security of a war against Iraq. There would be "an explosion of outrage against us" that "could well destabilize Arab regimes" and "could even swell the ranks of the terrorists."[12]

Even some military analysts did not share the rosy conservative predictions of Iraqis greeting the invaders as liberators. A report out of the U.S. Army War College that appeared a month before the invasion anticipated an eventual shift in Iraqi opinion toward their erstwhile liberators: "If the war is rapid with few casualties, the occupation will probably be characterized by an initial honeymoon period during which the United States will reap the benefits of ridding the population of a brutal dictatorship. Nevertheless, most Iraqis and most other Arabs will probably assume that the United States intervened in Iraq for its own reasons and not to liberate the population. Long-term gratitude is unlikely and suspicion of U.S. motives will increase as the occupation continues. A force initially viewed as liberators can rapidly be relegated to the status of invaders should an unwelcome occupation continue for a prolonged time. Occupation problems may be especially acute if the United States must implement the bulk of the occupation itself rather than turn these duties over to a postwar international force."[13] That conclusion was prescient.

To these realist arguments, the conservatives could merely sputter in rage and shout their claims through the mass media. The best arguments for war came not from these rants, but from Kenneth Pollack's book titled *The Threatening Storm: The Case for Invading Iraq*.[14] Pollack pointed out that Saddam, like Hitler and other megalomaniacs, at once grossly inflated his own power and dismissed the will and capability of his enemies. These delusions had most notably led to Iraq's disastrous war against Iran and its even more devastating defeat in the Gulf War. Nonetheless, Saddam at least learned something from those tragic blunders. He admitted that his biggest mistake was to invade Kuwait before he had nuclear weapons—with them he believed he would have deterred President George H. W. Bush from building a coalition and warring against him. He vowed never to make that mistake again. Saddam, whose greatest hero was Stalin, would be happy to die in his bunker with the knowledge that history would forever recall his rule and his nuclear attack on the American invaders. Indeed, the more people—foreigners and Iraqis alike—who died in that war, the more glorious his demise. Thus, facing such a pathological leader and a nearly inevitable war, then it was better to attack Saddam now when he had no nuclear weapons.

The realists agreed with Pollack's psychological assessment of Saddam. However, they countered that to attack a country now because it might acquire the means and will to attack the United States in the future was at best dubious on practical grounds and would clearly violate international law. Preemption is legal only against a pending attack, which Iraq had absolutely no ability or reason to make. The Gulf War and subsequent inspections had destroyed Iraq's offensive capacity for both its conventional military and WMDs.

Even if Saddam somehow retained or rebuilt an arsenal of mass destruction, would he use them against an enemy? During the war with Iran, the Iraqis had launched numerous chemical attacks via artillery shells, bombs, and missiles. Saddam also used chemical weapons to crush a Kurdish revolt in 1988, murdering at least five thousand civilians. Yet the knowledge that the United States would destroy him and his regime if he attacked American troops deterred him from doing so with his battle-ready WMDs during the Gulf War. Saddam would thus unblinkingly wield such weapons against the weak but would hesitate to launch them against the United States, unless his regime was threatened with destruction. Saddam hoped that the belief that he retained some chemical and biological weapons would deter an American attack against Iraq. That strategy had appeared to work in the Gulf War when Bush senior called off the war after liberating Kuwait.

The worst consequence of attacking Iraq would be to vastly empower America's enemies everywhere, especially Al Qaeda and other Islamist terrorist groups. They would rejoice at the modern-day crusader destroying an Arab regime, imposing a puppet regime, and letting America's corporate giants control its economy and oil. Thousands of mujahideen would converge on Iraq to kill the Americans and their allies or would try to topple pro-Western Arab regimes.

In sum, the case against warring against Iraq was simple: it would be a strategic, economic, and moral disaster for the United States.

ROUND TWO:
SHOCK AND AWE

"Let us not open a Pandora's Box."
—DOMINIQUE DE VILLEPIN

"Better forty years of dictatorship than one day of anarchy."
—ARAB SAYING

"The challenge for CIA analysts was not so much in predicting what the Iraqis would do. Where we ran into trouble was in our inability to foresee some of the actions of our own government."
—GEORGE TENET

"Even with a victory we believe that the medical, economic, environmental, moral, spiritual, political, and legal consequences of any American preventive war on Iraq would undermine, not protect, U.S. security and standing in the world."
—FORTY-ONE AMERICAN NOBEL LAUREATES

"What is going to happen the first time we hold an election in Iraq and it turns out the radicals win?"
—BRENT SCOWCROFT

"Freedom's untidy. And free people are free to make mistakes and commit crimes."
—DONALD RUMSFELD

"It turns out that we were all wrong. . . . Why could we all be so wrong?"
—WEAPONS INSPECTOR DAVID KAY

9

Planning "Shock and Awe"

Emboldened by the swift rout of the Taliban and Al Qaeda in Afghanistan, the conservatives reasoned that the American military would inflict as decisive and humiliating a victory not just over Saddam's regime, but also over all the naysayers who opposed their crusade. Deputy National Security Adviser Wayne Downing captured that mind-set when he confidently predicted that the United States would topple Saddam with air strikes and special operations forces alone, just like in Afghanistan. Indeed, as they drummed up support for the war against Iraq, the conservatives were already psyching themselves up for the next war after that. "Everyone wants to go to Baghdad," they jubilantly quipped, "but real men want to go to Tehran."

The realists were anything but sanguine. First they explained that the war in Afghanistan was far from over. The Americans had routed but not destroyed the Taliban and Al Qaeda. Sooner or later these Islamist forces would regroup, replant themselves, and spread across Afghanistan unless the country were blanketed with troops and aid workers to secure the population and develop the economy. They then accused the ideologues of naively assuming that what appeared to work well in one war would work just as well in another. A war in Iraq would turn out to be nothing like the war in Afghanistan. Whereas the Taliban and Al Qaeda forces probably numbered about thirty-five thousand armed men scattered on various fronts, the Iraqi army numbered at least a quarter million troops—perhaps twice that number. In Afghanistan the Northern Alliance had at least ten thousand warriors hardened by years of fighting; all they needed was an influx of military aid and advisers, along with American precision bombing, to rout the enemy entrenched before them. In Iraq there was no armed opposition, while most of the exiled members of the Iraqi National Congress had no intention of disrupting their affluent lives to war against Saddam; the closest front most would visit was their radio station in London.

Most important, a second war against Iraq would be nothing like the first. During the Gulf War the Iraqi army was entrenched in the desert where it endured thirty-nine days of bombing before being crushed in a four-day ground attack. Any second war would be fought house to house in Iraq's crowded cities. Baghdad alone had five million people and was defended by four Republican Guard divisions on the outskirts, and the Special Republican Guard division in the center, or 100,000 troops backed by tens of thousands of militiamen. With their survival at stake, Saddam, his equally sadistic sons Uday and Qusay, and most high-ranking Ba'ath Party officials would fight to the death.

And these were not the only caveats. Winning the war would be tough enough. Winning the peace would be far more challenging. How could the United States impose order, let alone democracy, on a hodgepodge, Texas-sized country of 24 million people split among three mutually hateful populations—Sunni, Shiite, and Kurd—which were in turn split among hundreds of tribes and thousands of clans? The conservative crusade would bog the United States down in a quagmire of worsening death, destruction, poverty, rage, and insurgency. Iraq would become a magnet for Islamists from around the world who were eager to kill Americans. Hundreds of billions of dollars and thousands of lives would be squandered in Iraq in a war that actually empowered America's enemies. And even if the United States were able to impose a democracy on Iraq, what would the Bush White House do if the people elected to power an anti-Western Islamist government? Defense Secretary Rumsfeld led the conservative counterattack against the realists for whom his most diplomatic epithet was "defeatist." He was determined to make the Iraq War a model of a new theory of warfare called the Revolution in Military Affairs (RMA), by which rapidly moving, small numbers of troops were armed with the most technologically cutting-edge

weapons and equipment and were supported by real-time intelligence and
smart-missiles and bombs. The result of that blitzkrieg of firepower and
movement would devastate Iraq's army and regime, and thus "shock and
awe" the enemy into swift capitulation. The key was to unleash three thousand precision-guided bombs and missiles on the command-and-control
system during the first forty-eight hours of combat, ten times more than
during the same time frame of the Gulf War. The hope was to implode the
regime so that the subsequent American units racing through the desert and
into Baghdad would be met along the way by surrendering Iraqi troops and
cheering Iraqi civilians.

Rumsfeld was hell bent on realizing his vision. He demanded on six different occasions that the Pentagon cut back the number of troops that it insisted were essential for destroying the regime and securing Iraq. He was
deaf to those who tried to explain that the United States would actually need
more "boots on the ground" after vanquishing the Iraqi army, in order to
maintain order. The generals retreated before Rumsfeld's demands. Gen.
Tommy Franks, the theater commander, and his advisers had originally
wanted at least a quarter million troops and two weeks of bombing. Rumsfeld
eventually forced him to pare down to a hundred and fifty thousand troops
and a bombing campaign that accompanied the ground offensive.[1]

There was at least one political casualty along the way. A month before
the invasion, Army Chief of Staff Gen. Eric Shinseki told Congress that "several hundred thousand" troops would be necessary to take and hold Iraq.
This statement provoked a conservative uproar, and Shinseki was forced
into an early retirement.

The invasion's success might have had as much to do with the weather as
anything else. The best time for war in Iraq was February, with its long nights
and cool days. With its ability to see and shoot in the dark, the American
military would fight and move mostly at night and then rest during the day.
The threat of an Iraqi chemical attack made cool weather all the more essential, since the Americans would have to encase themselves in heavy protective
suits at the first possibility of deadly agents. This was why the Bush team
was so eager to launch the war as soon as possible and why those who opposed the war wanted to delay the invasion as long as possible, hoping that
the onset of hot weather would force the war's indefinite postponement.

Rumsfeld's vision of rapid military victory would be fulfilled. But that victory depended to a great extent on the intelligence, sabotage, bombing, and propaganda war that actually began at least a year before the invasion. In the "Southern Focus" campaign from the summer of 2002 until March 2003, the U.S. Air Force and Navy flew 21,736 sorties over Iraq, during which it dropped 696 bombs on 391 sites. The Iraqis fired 651 times without any effect other than to reveal their locations and other useful intelligence. The result was that Iraq's systems for command, control, communications, and intelligence (C³I) and for logistics were devastated before the invasion began.[2]

Meanwhile special operations teams of troops and CIA operatives infiltrated Iraq to gather intelligence and enlist allies. As early as February 2002, the CIA's Northern Iraq Liaison Element began mobilizing Kurds and other disaffected groups to rise against Saddam's regime. Eventually over nine thousand special operations troops were deployed in strategic points around Iraq. When the U.S. military invaded southern Iraq, these elite warriors would call in surgical air strikes or emerge from their hidden lairs to eliminate nearby enemy forces and installations.[3]

All along, the Americans waged psychological warfare. U.S. aircraft dropped eight million leaflets urging the Iraqis to surrender, while the CIA got more personal by sending e-mails and cell phone calls to twenty-nine military leaders in southern Iraq alone, and to scores of others elsewhere in the country. Radio programs of music and propaganda were broadcasted by EC-130E planes flying over the country.[4]

By late March there were more than 248,000 American, 45,000 British, 1,000 Australian, and 500 Polish soldiers, and 1,000 warplanes and 100 warships in the Gulf theater. About 130,000 American, 25,000 British, and all the Australians were coiled in Kuwait, while many of the Poles were among the special operations forces that had slipped into Iraq.

These were the front-line troops. The paper strength of the Bush administration's "coalition of the willing" totaled 297,000 troops, although only six of the forty-nine governments in the coalition publicly declaring their support for the war actually contributed troops, and of the six only the United States and Britain donated more than token numbers. The 248,000 American troops represented 83 percent of the total, followed by Britain with 45,000

(15 percent), South Korea with 3,500 (1.1 percent), Australia with 2,000 (0.6 percent), Denmark with 200 (0.06 percent), and Poland with 184 (0.06 percent). Thirty-three countries would later contribute troops, again mostly in token numbers.

Powerful as those forces were, they could have been even more so. The biggest disappointment was the diplomatic failure with Ankara. The Turks refused to let the coalition invade northern Iraq from their territory. Had they done so, the allies could have simultaneously attacked Iraq from south and north, and thus caught the enemy in a giant vise. With the ground attack now confined to fighting from Kuwait northward, the Iraqis had more opportunity to concentrate their forces. But it turned out that this had little effect on the war.

On paper the estimated strength of the Iraqi ground forces was formidable. In all there were 375,000 regular soldiers, 44,000 paramilitary troops, and 80,000 Republican Guards, backed by 675,000 reserves. The actual figures were far fewer. The vast majority would desert soon after the bombs began to drop or surrender to the first American or British troops who appeared.

Donald Rumsfeld's vision of a dazzling blitzkrieg against Iraq would be brilliantly realized.

10

Unleashing "Shock and Awe"

President Bush made the decision to unleash the blitzkrieg on March 19 during a meeting with his inner circle in the White House's Situation Room. The discussion began at 3:40 that afternoon, and Bush announced his decision around 6:30. The timing was prompted by reports that the Iraqis were igniting their oil fields.

That dramatic decision was swiftly followed by another even more so. The war would open with an attempt to decapitate Iraq's leadership. The CIA received word from an agent in Saddam's inner circle pinpointing where the dictator, his two sons, and other prominent leaders were hunkered down. Bush agreed at 7:12 to a plan to destroy that command post with two-thousand-pound bunker-buster bombs dropped by F-117 stealth ground-attack aircraft, along with three dozen Tomahawk cruise missiles. Although the target was destroyed, the fate of the tyrant and his brutal sons would not be known for days thereafter. Three hours later, at 10:15, Bush made his televised Oval Office speech announcing that the war had begun.

The following day, March 20, Congress overwhelmingly approved the war, with the Senate voting 99 to 0 and the House 392 to 11. The American public was more divided. A *New York Times*/CBS poll that day found 62 percent agreed with the attack while 35 percent believed that the inspectors should have been given more time. For the White House the downside was that 59 percent of Americans thought the invasion made a terrorist retaliatory attack on the United States more likely, while only 8 percent thought the risk had decreased.[1]

This proportion of two-thirds of Americans supporting the war and one-third opposing it would persist for another year. Although antiwar protests erupted in scores of cities across the United States, none reached the massive numbers in Europe and elsewhere. The overwhelming public support for the war can be explained by the "rally-around-the-flag" syndrome by which even the most informed and free-thinking Americans give a president the benefit of the doubt when the bombs start to drop. Compounding that was the swift destruction of Saddam's army and regime, the conservatives' skilful manipulation of the mass media, and the ignorance of most Americans of the mounting violence, anarchy, and anti-Americanism that followed as soon as the "shock and awe" wore off.

To best spin its war, the Bush administration "embedded" hundreds of journalists at all levels of the war effort; the camaraderie forged between the journalists and the soldiers resulted in front-line stories of courage and sac-rifice rather than bird's-eye views that might have asked tough questions and revealed mistakes, atrocities, and corruption. The Pentagon paid $1.5 million for a state-of-the-art set for the media briefings of Gen. Tommy Franks at his Qatar headquarters.[2]

Leading what would be for years a hyperpatriotic reporting romp was the Fox News Corporation, owned by conservative spokesman and Bush administration adviser Roger Ailes. The "Foxification" of America's mass media was evident in the war's coverage. Most print and electronic stories described operations instead of analyzing the war's broader international context and consequences. Moreover, these stories tended to be packaged in red, white, and blue bunting rather than in cool objectivity. Only Peter Jennings, the ABC News anchor, approached the professional standards of the BBC. Conservatives pilloried him.

The air and ground war unfolded tightly with the initial strategy. In the first barrage the air force and navy launched hundreds of precision-guided bombs and missiles on Iraq's C³I and logistical sites that had not previously been targeted during the previous months attacks. Over the next three weeks, about eighteen hundred allied aircraft launched twenty thousand strikes, of which about fifteen thousand were directed against Iraq's military, eighteen hundred against the government, and eight hundred against sus-pected caches of WMDs.[3]

Although that bombardment did not kill Saddam or immediately collapse his regime, it devastated Iraq's military and government infrastructure. As the initial barrage was unleashed, troops rushed to secure Iraq's Rumallah oil fields from destruction. Luckily the Iraqis ignited only six of the 1,685 wells, a sliver compared to the 603 they torched and 100 others they damaged in Kuwait during the Gulf War.[4]

Within two days American and British troops had secured Iraq's sole seaport of Umm Qasr and opened it to allied shipping. The U.S. Army Third Division and the U.S. Marine Corps First Division then raced up the Euphrates and Tigris valleys, respectively, while the U.S. 101st Airborne Division dropped at strategic points along both routes, and the British besieged Basra. In northern Iraq, a joint offensive by special operations forces, the U.S. 173rd Airborne Brigade, and Kurds routed a militant group known as Ansar al-Islam led by Abu Musaab al-Zarqawi.

Iraqi resistance was sporadic at best. With American air superiority, most Iraqi troops could do little more than huddle in their bunkers and pray that they escaped death. When ordered to attack, often at gunpoint, they were mowed down by coalition troops. At best, small groups of regular troops or militiamen sniped and then slipped away.

Saddam himself fed the debacle. Instead of drawing his units into the cities for "hedgehog defenses" and street-to-street resistance, he left most of them out in the open where they were pulverized. He did not blow up key bridges and dams, which would have slowed the coalition's advance. Yet, even had he taken these measures, his army could have at best held on a few more bloody weeks.

The invasion was slowed more by the weather than by Iraqis. During the first week a sandstorm stalled most ground operations for a couple of days. By April temperatures exceeded 100 degrees, and more soldiers were downed by heat exhaustion than by Iraqi bullets and mines. Supply was also a problem. The campaign daily consumed about 15 million gallons of fuel along with munitions, food, and other essentials.

As for all the Scuds and WMDs that the Bush team had claimed Saddam was prepared to fire, they proved to be a mirage. In the first days of fighting, the Iraqis did launch two surface-to-surface missiles known as the Abadil-100s, along with a Chinese-made Seersucker antiship missile. Patriot missiles reputedly destroyed the two Abadils, while the Seersucker narrowly missed an American base.

So what happened to all the WMDs that the Bush administration had insisted Iraq possessed, thus justifying the American onslaught? Although Saddam held chemical and biological weapons in the Gulf War, he was then deterred from using them by the threat of overwhelming American retaliation, which would have destroyed both him and his regime. But deterrence worked both ways. A key reason why President George H. W. Bush did not invade Iraq was the knowledge that Saddam would unleash those WMDs if he himself was threatened with extinction.

Now, with nothing left to lose, Saddam would logically empty his arsenal. But the tyrant did not do that. While conservatives puzzled over that mystery, realists explained that this could only mean that his arsenal was empty. This came as no surprise to many experts on Iraq. Scott Ritter, who had led inspection teams during the 1990s, was the most outspoken of those who said that Iraq's WMDs no longer existed. For years he and many of his colleagues had explained that the combination of the Gulf War, postwar inspections, and decisions by Saddam himself had resulted in the destruction of Iraq's chemical and biological weapons. But of course this was not the message that conservatives wanted to hear.[5]

Even if a few of those weapons still existed, most would likely have deteriorated to the point of being useless. Most chemical and biological weapons have shelf lives and must be maintained or else they expire. And even if there were still a few technically useable weapons squirreled away, any Iraqi attempt to fire them would backfire both literally and diplomatically. The weapons would be fired at targets within Iraq and more likely kill and maim Iraqis rather than the invaders. The diplomatic damage might even be worse as the Bush administration could crow to the world "We told you so!" Hans Blix pointed out that if the Iraqis still had any chemical or biological weapons, he "would doubt they would use [them] because a lot of countries and peoples in the world are negative to the idea. . . . And if the Iraqis were to use any . . . weapons then . . . the public around the world will immediately turn against the Iraqis." But if Iraq's WMDs were not wielded during the war, they could be detonated elsewhere by others. There were unsubstantiated reports that weapons were being smuggled out of Iraq to neighboring friendly states or terrorist groups.[6]

A controversy over strategy erupted despite the coalition's dazzling advance against sporadic resistance. The conservatives had raised naive hopes, which many commanders were eager to point out. In the week before the invasion, Vice President Cheney had boasted that "the streets in Basra and Baghdad are sure to erupt in joy" as the Iraqi army "cracked like peanut brittle." Richard Perle, who chaired the Defense Policy Board, was just as Pollyannaish: "Support for Saddam, including within his military organization, will collapse with the first whiff of gun smoke."[7]

Lt. Gen. William Wallace, the ground commander, complained that the enemy "was different from the one we war-gamed against." That statement initiated a chorus of criticism led most prominently by retired generals Wesley Clark, Joseph Hoar, and Barry McCaffrey, the respective former commanders of NATO, the Central Command, and a division in the Gulf War. Hoar argued that the invasion force lacked the number of troops for conquering a country "with poor weather; long vulnerable supply lines; an enemy that decides to fight; an undecided if not downright hostile civilian population; and the use of guerilla tactics." He deplored the Pentagon's civilian leaders who ridiculed for their "old thinking" those in uniform who had advocated more troops. To McCaffrey the Bush administration strategy's key "problem is that they chose to attack 250 miles into Iraq with one armored division and no rear area security and no second front."[8]

Rumsfeld revealed his true character by ducking the controversy and blaming Gen. Tommy Franks, the theater commander, for the plan, which had then been approved by the Joint Chiefs of Staff. The defense secretary insisted that he had played only a devil's advocate role in making the plan. That claim runs counter to the leading published accounts of the war planning. The Bush team did not simply defend the plan—they launched a typical smear attack on its critics, questioning not just their arguments but their patriotism.

This time the targets were not Democrats or moderate Republicans, most of whom were by now thoroughly cowed by years of McCarthyite tactics by conservatives in the White House, Congress, and the mainstream media. The dissidents were men who had actually fought for their country, an experience confined among Bush's inner circle only to Secretary of State Powell and his deputy Richard Armitage, both realists.

Yet the dissidents refused to abandon their First Amendment rights and fought back against administrative bullying. McCaffrey was especially outspoken about the essential American right to speak freely: "This war is too important to be left to the secretary [Rumsfeld] alone. At the end of the day I think they ought to value public opinion."[9]

But while the critics were right about the Constitution, they were wrong about the war strategy. The White House's initial plan and subsequent shifts with the fortunes of war were brilliant in conception and execution. There is no evidence that with more boots on the ground the offensive would have advanced any faster; indeed the advance might have slowed as those extra troops gobbled more supplies. True, the Bush team deluded themselves and the public with the belief that they would be greeted as liberators while the Iraqi masses turned on Saddam's regime. But militarily this belief made no difference to the outcome.

The debate was actually more about politics than strategy. To his credit, Rumsfeld did try to transform the military from a late twentieth-century fighting force into a twenty-first-century one by deploying appropriate high technology at all levels to make American forces swifter, deadlier, and more knowledgeable about the enemy. That often meant eliminating obsolete weapons and equipment, and reducing heavy armor and artillery units, and increasingly relying on drones rather than pilots in the air. Those essential reforms, however, threatened many traditional career paths and budgets for each service, especially the army, whose officers grumbled the loudest. Moreover, Rumsfeld's imperious personality rubbed salt into the proposed cuts.

An international diplomatic offensive accompanied the blitzkrieg in Iraq but was less successful. The State Department asked the host governments to expel three hundred Iraqi intelligence agents working under diplomatic cover in sixty-two countries around the world. In the end only Jordan and Italy kicked out their suspects; the other countries, including traditional allies, spurned the request. The White House did succeed in lining up enough allies on the UN Human Rights Commission to reject a proposal to investigate alleged American abuses in Iraq. Twenty-five countries voted against and eighteen for the resolution, while seven abstained and three were absent.[10]

The Bush administration issued stern warnings to countries secretly aiding Iraq and committing "hostile acts" against the United States. Bush telephoned President Vladimir Putin and demanded that he halt sales by Russian companies. Putin sidestepped the question by citing the value of free markets and the fears of a humanitarian disaster unfolding in Iraq. Rumsfeld threatened unspecified repercussions if the Syrians did not stop selling night-vision and other military equipment to Iraq. He warned Tehran not to allow the Badr Corps of Iraqi exiles, which was trained, equipped, and directed by Iran's Islamic Revolutionary Guards, to enter Iraq.[11]

After rejecting the use of its territory for a northern front against Iraq, Turkey's parliament approved on March 19 a bill that opened the nation's airspace to American aircraft. Powell tried to follow that concession and repair some of the earlier diplomatic damage with a visit to Ankara on April 1. In return for a promise of a $1 billion grant and an $8 billion loan, Prime Minister Erdoğan agreed to allow the United States to send relief supplies overland through Turkey to Iraq. Erdoğan maintained that since the supplies were nonlethal, he would not need parliament's approval. Turkey had over forty thousand troops deployed just north of the border and several thousand in a twelve-mile buffer zone in northern Iraq. Erdoğan promised not to send more troops into northern Iraq unless a humanitarian disaster or war erupted among the Kurdish clans. Over forty thousand Turkish troops were deployed just north of the border with Iraq.[12]

The conservatives typically scapegoated France for blocking the White House's Security Council resolution that would have authorized the invasion. There was some retaliation, although only a fraction of what had been threatened. The largest was when the Pentagon canceled a $1 billion contract with the French food services company Sodexho Alliance to supply the Marine Corps. Eighteen members of the House of Representatives sponsored a resolution that would have forced American firms to boycott the Paris Air Show, an event that in 2002 had earned sales of $60 billion for the eighteen hundred exhibiters, 36.7 percent of which funds went to American companies. Fortunately for the American wealth and power that would be augmented by sales at the show, the measure did not pass. In a typically silly, childish gesture, congressional conservatives did succeed in getting the House cafeteria to rename French fries "freedom fries."[13]

Despite those acts the French offered an olive branch of sorts. Foreign Minister Villepin argued that "these times of great changes call for a renewed close trusting relationship with the United States." He predicted that "because they share common values, the United States and France will reestablish close cooperation in complete solidarity." Yet he warned that the Bush Doctrine of conquering countries that might one day be threats risks "introducing the principle of constant instability and uncertainty" into international relations. "Let us not open a Pandora's Box." He finally called on the United States and all nations to work for peace through the United Nations. The Bush administration pointedly ignored that call for reconciliation.[14]

After three weeks of war, the Americans had overrun much of Iraq and had punched into districts of Baghdad itself. Organized large-scale resistance had ceased. Iraq's leadership was either dead or in hiding. Thousands of Iraqi soldiers had been killed; tens of thousands surrendered or donned civilian clothes and tried to get home. The shootings and violence grew more sporadic. More people ventured into the streets to welcome the invaders and ask for handouts.

Even if the conservative crusade in Iraq was unjust by any practical, legal, or moral measure, America's military certainly fought it justly. The Pentagon used all the high technology and tactical means at its disposal to minimize civilian casualties. Militarily the war was a dazzling success. Rumsfeld's vision of a war combining cutting-edge technologies, pinpoint bombing, and special operations forces destroying the enemy from their rear while heavy divisions smashed through and dashed forward was vindicated. The strategy of simultaneously launching air and ground assaults was brilliantly conceived and executed. Within three weeks the coalition destroyed nearly all significant resistance outside of the capital, raced to Baghdad's outskirts, and secured a 350-mile supply line from the Persian Gulf, while suffering only several hundred casualties. American troops first entered Baghdad on April 9 and declared the city secure on April 14.

Bush's handlers devised an ingenuous photo op to symbolize and celebrate the "victory" in Iraq. On May 1, 2003, a large crowd of the Republican Party elite, sailors, and reporters packed atop the aircraft carrier USS *Abraham Lincoln*. Hanging from the control tower was a huge banner emblazoned with the words "Mission Accomplished." An S-3B Viking reconnaissance plane skimmed across San Diego bay toward the carrier and screeched to a half on the deck. George W. Bush emerged, dressed in a flight suit, grinning, and cradling his helmet. The excited viewers could be forgiven if they believed that the president himself had piloted the plane onto the carrier.

George W. Bush announced to the wildly cheering crowd that "major combat operations in Iraq have ended. In the battle of Iraq, the United States and its allies have prevailed."

It was in many ways the exhilarating high point of his presidency. Tragically, in reality, the war had only just begun.

11
Picking Up the Pieces

On April 10, 2003, three symbolic acts marked the end of Saddam Hussein's regime and foreshadowed an uncertain future for Iraq. In a televised speech subtitled in Arabic, President Bush reminded the Iraqis that they were "the heirs of a great civilization that contributes to humanity." Meanwhile in Baghdad's central plaza, Americans and Iraqis toppled a huge statue of Saddam; an American flag briefly draped his face. But elsewhere in Baghdad, looters broke into the national archeological museum and national library, stealing and smashing priceless works of art and ancient texts from one of humanity's oldest civilizations.

The immediate effect of the conservative crusade in Iraq was not freedom but anarchy. Mobs rampaged through the streets, pillaging seventeen of twenty-three government ministries along with warehouses, private homes, businesses, museums, and, most ominously, weapon depots. A nationwide inventory completed by October 2004 revealed that as many as a quarter million tons of munitions were missing. Insurgents were soon wielding those guns and bombs against the American invaders and their foreign and Iraqi allies. Ironically one of the devastated bureaucracies—the National Monitoring Directorate—may have held critical records on Iraq's WMD program.[1]

All that destruction and violence did not faze the conservatives. When asked whether the anarchy reflected a lack of foresight and preparation by the administration, Rumsfeld offered this comforting wisdom: "Freedom's untidy. And free people are free to make mistakes and commit crimes." The contrast of Rumsfeld's dismissal of the devastation of Iraq's heritage with the words of Gen. Dwight Eisenhower on the eve of D-Day could not have been starker. Eisenhower explained: "Inevitably in the path of our advance will be found historical monuments and cultural centers which symbolize to the world all that we are fighting to preserve. It is the responsibility of every commander to protect and respect these symbols whenever possible."[2]

Most Iraqis were noticeably ungrateful to the Americans for their "liberation." Within days of Baghdad's fall, mass anti-American demonstrations of Sunnis and Shiites erupted in the capital and a dozen other cities; they demanded that the foreign invaders leave Iraq. Pockets of insurgents sniped and launched bombs against the invaders and their collaborators.

The CIA had anticipated this anarchy in an analysis entitled "The Perfect Storm: Planning for Negative Consequences of Invading Iraq," issued on August 13, 2002, seven months before the invasion. Tragically the CIA was unable to convince the White House of this pending anarchy nor how to deal with it. As CIA Director Tenet later wistfully expressed the dilemma: "The challenge for CIA analysts was not so much in predicting what the Iraqis would do. Where we ran into trouble was in our inability to foresee some of the actions of our own government."[3]

Consumed with planning for the invasion and ideologically contemptuous of "nation-building," the administration could at best produce only the sketchiest of notions for Iraq's postwar fate. Bush issued an order on January 20, 2003, that the Pentagon would run Iraq after Saddam's regime was destroyed. The hope was that the occupation would last only a half year before an interim Iraqi government took over. Reality would crush that naive hope, as it would so many others cherished by the conservatives.

To pile one absurdity upon another, the State Department and CIA had not only predicted all the postwar chaos and violence, they had devised an elaborate plan and shadow government to run the country known as "the Future of Iraq Project." Beginning nearly a year before the invasion, they gathered more than two hundred Iraqi lawyers, businessmen, engineers, technicians, educators, administrators, and others, and divided them among seventeen groups that spanned the range of postwar political, economic, social, educational, environmental, religious, and security problems. They anticipated and prepared for all the disasters that subsequently unfolded during the war, including the destruction of basic infrastructure such as the electrical grid, water supplies, health care, and garbage disposal; the widespread looting of the ministries, museums, and shops; and the insurgency. To support the Iraq administration, the State Department's Agency for International Development (AID) and Office of Foreign Disaster Assistance (OFDA) would deploy Disaster Assistance Response Teams (DARTs) across Iraq where they were most needed. The final report was a two-thousand-page blueprint for developing Iraq from mass poverty and oppression into prosperity and democracy.[4]

So why were not that plan and the shadow administration made the foundation for governing postwar Iraq? Ideology and politics once again trumped common sense and American national interests. First, the plan came from those bastions of realism, the State Department and the CIA, rather than the Pentagon or White House. Second, the plan rejected any significant role for Ahmed Chalabi and his INC, darlings of the conservatives. Third, bureaucratic politics demanded that the Pentagon try to expand its power, prestige, and budget as far as possible at the expense of its rivals. Finally, Defense Secretary Rumsfeld's egomania demanded nothing less. As a result, Bush rejected the Future of Iraq Project and instead authorized the Pentagon to create an entirely new organization and plan for running postwar Iraq just two months before the invasion.

The Pentagon refused to accept any analysis or advice from the State Department and CIA. Rumsfeld and his staff based their "planning" on a polar opposite set of assumptions that the Americans would be greeted as liberators, that damage to people, property, and infrastructure along with population displacement would be limited, that oil revenues would soon pay for reconstruction and a post-Saddam government, and that there would be no insurgency. They were tragically wrong about all those assumptions.

The reason is clear enough. Blinded by their ideology, the conservatives consistently misunderstood history and made these misunderstandings either the foundation of, or justification for, their policies. For instance, they claimed that the American occupation of Iraq would be as successful in transforming that country from aggressive authoritarianism into a peaceful and prosperous democracy as were the American occupations of Japan and Germany following

World War II. This comparison does not hold up to historical scrutiny. First of all, the planning for the occupations of Japan and Germany began more than two and a half years before the defeat of those countries and involved the joint, coordinated efforts of the State, War, and Navy departments. Second, Japan and Germany had developed into democracies and middle-class economies before turning to fascism in the 1930s. So that once the fascist institutions were demolished, the Americans could root their sweeping reforms in genuine political and economic development. Iraq, in contrast, was an authoritarian petrostate whose people had never experienced liberalism.

Controlling, let alone developing, Iraq would be a nearly impossible challenge under the best of circumstances. Even before the 2003 invasion, Iraq's economy was a shambles. That benighted country had experienced war and/or sanctions virtually every year since 1980. The diversion of hundreds of billions of dollars for Iraq's war with Iran and then the Gulf War was self-destructive enough. The economic sanctions were even more economically devastating. In August 1990 the Security Council issued the first of eventually sixteen resolutions that straight-jacketed Iraq's economy. From 1990 to 1996, there was a total embargo on Iraqi oil and other exports. Unable to earn money, Iraq racked up enormous debts to foreign lenders that amounted to over $120 billion in 2003.

Since its inauguration in 1996, the United Nation's oil-for-food program had kept starvation at bay for about 16 million of Iraq's 24 million people. The program controlled Iraq's oil sales and put the profit into an account that was used to purchase goods from a list of essential products. With $2.9 billion in escrow, the program was suspended when the invasion began.

The Gulf War was the most punishing economic divide. Before the coalition bombing campaign of 1991, 95 percent of people in the cities and 75 percent of rural dwellers enjoyed running water, but the bombings and sanctions steadily diminished that flow. By 2000 the daily average water consumption had plummeted from 330 liters to 150 liters in Baghdad, from 270 liters to 110 liters in other cities, and from 180 liters to 65 liters in the countryside. Iraq's economy officially generated only $12.3 billion of income, while its foreign debt was over $125 billion.[5]

Iraq had achieved considerable economic development before the series of wars beginning in 1980 shattered the country. Iraq is heavily urbanized, with eight of ten people living in cities with more than 50,000 people. The transportation and communication systems are also highly developed. Iraq's population is quite literate for the Middle East, with 74 percent of adults able to read and write (84 percent of males and 64 percent of females).

Amidst countless smaller ones, Iraq has two major cleavages. One is ethnic, with Iraq's population split among 75 to 80 percent who are Arabs, 15 to 20 percent who are Kurds, and perhaps as many as 5 percent who are Turks. Then there is the religious divide among the approximately 60 percent of the population who are Shiite, the nearly 40 percent who are Sunni, and the 1 or 2 percent who are Christians or follow some other religion.

Of those two cleavages, religion has been the most deadly. For over thirteen centuries, theological differences between Sunnis and Shiites have sparked constant tension and frequent violence. Only a powerful state has suppressed the violence that is rooted in those ancient hatreds.

Corruption permeated virtually all of Iraq's political, economic, and social institutions. From its 1963 coup, the socialist Ba'ath Party had brutally ruled and exploited Iraq. The party was modeled on a communist party hierarchy of power whose cells extended into every corner of society. The Ba'ath party spied on virtually everyone, rewarded those who conformed, and meted out the vilest of punishments, including torture and murder, to those who dissented.

For foreign invaders Iraq does have some advantages. The country is mostly flat desert except for the hilly northern region. For foreign occupiers, however, the downside is that Iraq is heavily urbanized. Guerrillas can easily hide in the densely packed maze of buildings, markets, and teeming streets.

The initial institution for occupying Iraq was known as the Office of Reconstruction and Humanitarian Assistance (ORHA), led by retired general Jay Garner.[6] Garner was a good choice. He had led Operation Provide Comfort, which aided the Kurds after the Gulf War. But this time he was given a mission impossible. He only got the job on January 13, a mere two months before the invasion. He then had to race to set up ORHA with an organization, personnel, budget, and equipment, and then deploy it in the wake of the American invasion. As if those challenges were not overwhelming enough, Rumsfeld pettily denied Garner permission to employ State Department experts who had worked on the Future of Iraq Project.

Short of everything vital for the job, Garner and about 150 personnel set up shop in Baghdad on April 21. He and ORHA would not last long. In response to the worsening anarchy, looting, and violence, the Bush administration found a scapegoat to blame, as well as a savior to rescue the mission. On May 6 the president fired Garner and replaced him with L. Paul Bremer, a retired career diplomat and then director of Henry Kissinger's consulting group.

ORHA was renamed the Coalition Provisional Authority (CPA) and was charged with fulfilling four reconstruction "pillars": justice, security, infrastructure, and governance. To underwrite that agenda, the White House set up the Iraq Relief and Reconstruction Fund (IRRF) with an initial allocation of $2.5 billion. The CPA hunkered down and got to work in the Green Zone, a 3.8-square-mile district in the heart of Baghdad surrounded by a wall and guarded by thousands of troops.

The CPA would bungle all four of its missions, for many interrelated reasons. Within days of reaching Baghdad on May 12, Bremer committed the two most grievous mistakes, although with the White House's full approval. On May 16 he abolished the Ba'ath Party and purged members on its four highest levels from all public jobs. On May 23 he abolished all military, paramilitary, and intelligence forces.

The Bush administration's purge policy at once worsened the anarchy and vastly boosted the nascent insurgency's ranks and ferocity. The professional ranks of the ministries, industries, oil refineries, electrical plants, water and sewage systems, schools, hospitals, police, and other essential services were decimated. Few of those purged would have posed a threat to the occupation forces had they been left alone. Indeed most were members not from belief, but because the Ba'ath Party was the only road to enriching careers and status. Likewise most of the military and intelligence forces would have cooperated had they been treated with professional respect rather than abruptly shorn of their incomes, prestige, and pride. In all, the Bush team purged as many as fifty thousand Ba'athists and half a million members of the security forces. Now, with nothing to lose, countless numbers of former Ba'athists and soldiers began detonating bombs and firing guns against the invaders.[7]

Yet another self-defeating decision was to use ideological correctness rather than professional standards to fill the CPA's ranks. The Bush team hired and sent thousands of Americans to work for the CPA. The key to getting picked was to display Republican Party loyalty and to spout conservative platitudes. But zealotry could not make up for the lack of technical skills desperately needed to reconstruct Iraq. Meanwhile, waiting in the wings were a team of 737 experts, including eighty Arab linguists, from the State Department and CIA who had spent nearly a year preparing for the occupation. In an all too typical display of egomania and bureaucratic pettiness, Defense Secretary Rumsfeld barred that team from joining the CPA.[8]

In all, the American occupation of Iraq was off to a rocky start. It would soon descend into a maelstrom of violence.

12

Passing the Hat

Among the most pressing questions repeatedly asked by journalists and concerned members of Congress in the year leading up to the invasion and thereafter was just how much the Iraq War would cost America. The answers varied depending on the respondent's honesty. Before the invasion, General Shinseki told Congress that the first year's bill could be as high as $95 billion. The Bush administration reacted to the outcry against this vast expenditure of American power and wealth by forcing him to retire and trotting out spokesmen to downplay the costs and commitment. History has sustained Shinseki's appraisal.

Those who had demanded how much the war, occupation, and reconstruction would cost got the first concrete number on March 24, 2003, five days after the invasion began. Bush asked Congress for $74.7 billion, including $62.6 billion for the war, $4.24 billion for homeland security, $7.85 billion for short-term relief and reconstruction, and $1.4 billion for the allies. Nine days later Congress approved the request—the Senate unanimously and the House by 414 to 12—with the add-ons ratcheting up the cost for American taxpayers to $79 billion. But that bill would only cover expenses for the next six months and was atop the tens of billions of dollars that had already been spent in the buildup to the war.[1]

Six months later the knowing nodded wearily and the unwary gasped when Bush demanded another $87 billion to pay for the next fiscal year. When added to his previous bill for $79 billion, the conservative crusade's direct costs to America's taxpayers would be $166 billion for the first eighteen months alone. But that was just a down payment. The final bill would include not just the direct costs of fighting, but also the indirect costs of interest on the national debt, greater health care costs for the maimed, lost productivity as wealth was diverted from better investments elsewhere, and greater security costs as the Iraq War provoked rather than quelled terrorism.

To those who criticized all these unnecessary burdens, conservatives retorted that the war's costs were a small price to pay to prevent an Iraqi WMD attack on the United States. Besides, Iraqi oil sales would soon cover most of the costs. After all, as Paul Wolfowitz pointed out, "we are dealing with a country that can really finance its own reconstruction. . . . Oil revenues of that country could bring between $50 billion and $100 billion over the course of the next two or three years."[2]

In reality, that hope would prove to be a chimera over the short run and will be very difficult to achieve over the long run. Iraq's oil production had already fallen from 3.5 million barrels in 1980 to 2.8 million in 2003. Oil production then plummeted over the next few years because of sabotage and the insurgency. By the time the Bush team finally left office, the surge and the tens of billions of dollars in investments had brought production back only to its preinvasion capacity.

CPA chief Bremer was able to scrape up $5.4 billion from existing Iraqi accounts and foreign aid to pay for the salaries of the 2 million officials employed by twenty-three ministries and seventeen provincial governments. He also set up a Development Fund for Iraq with $1.5 billion and a Trade Bank of Iraq with $100 million in credits.[3]

These were just stopgap measures to paper over Iraq's immediate crisis over food and government salaries. The realists continued to insist that for the occupation to have any chance of success, the hat would have to be passed and a pitch made to every foreign government and international aid organization. On his own initiative, Secretary of State Powell got Prime Minster Blair, the European Union, and a spectrum of governmental and private humanitarian institutions to offer to assist the occupation.

Here again ideology trumped common sense. Miffed that the Europeans and others had rejected their war, the Bush team initially rejected their generous offer to share the burdens of winning the peace. Price, apparently, was no object to the conservatives in their zeal to make Iraq a showcase for their version of American power.[4]

The conservative "my way or the highway" obsession eventually got the better of them. The bills soared and started coming due. The occupation's initial cost of $3.9 billion a month rose steadily until it peaked at $10 billion a month in 2007. As the task of nation-building grew ever more onerous, the Bush administration grudgingly admitted that for some tasks multilateralism might just be better than going it alone. Eventually George W. Bush himself had to swallow a bit of his overweening hubris and call on the international financial community, hat in hand. The Bush team was especially eager to get its hands on the $10.3 billion in the United Nations' escrow account.

But the years in which Bush and his fellow conservatives repeatedly jabbed their fingers in the eyes of the international community came back to haunt them. Almost everywhere he and others on his team turned for help, they were politely but firmly turned away with the diplomatic equivalents of "we told you so" and "you broke it, you fix it." The leaders of the World Bank, International Monetary Fund (IMF), and a host of other potential donors explained that legally their hands were tied unless the White House got the Security Council to approve the war and occupation. Only "recognized governments" are eligible for debt write-offs, reschedulings, and aid programs.

So Bush demanded that the Security Council end economic sanctions on Iraq and release money from the escrow account to pay for the American occupation. The foreign ministers of Iraq's neighbors—Saudi Arabia, Turkey, Iran, Kuwait, and Jordan—along with Egypt and Bahrain, opposed any lifting of sanctions until a legitimate government of Iraqis took power in Baghdad.[5] Those who assumed that France would automatically join that chorus, however, were surprised. The French stood on their long-standing principle that the sanctions only hurt the Iraqi people and thus should be lifted. Was this the first step toward a reconciliation of differences? The Bush team did not see it that way. A spokesperson rather bizarrely and pettily described France's acceptance of Bush's demand as "maybe a move, you know, sort of in the right direction."[6]

On May 23 the White House achieved a vital diplomatic victory. After twelve days of debate, the Security Council approved, with Syria's abstention,

Resolution 1483, which lifted sanctions, authorized the United States and Britain to manage Iraq's reconstruction, and called on all UN members to assist that effort. This allowed the United Nations to open its escrow account and the IMF to begin negotiating with Iraq for the restructuring of its debts. The only snag was when the World Bank said that it could only grant new loans after Iraq had a constitution and a new government.

That resolution also allowed the United Nations to return to Iraq. The Bush team welcomed that mission both as a sign of legitimacy for their occupation and a boost for reconstruction. Tragically, that UN mission did not last long. On August 19, 2003, a terrorist bomb destroyed the UN headquarters in Baghdad, killing Sérgio Vieira de Mello, the gifted mission chief, and twenty-one other workers. The United Nations promptly withdrew its mission.

On September 23, 2003, President Bush took his plea for money and troops before the UN General Assembly. As usual he was assertive rather than conciliatory, boasting of what he believed his policies had or would accomplish in Iraq and contemptuous of those who did not share his vision. In their respective speeches, Kofi Annan and Jacques Chirac spoke for most governments and much of humanity when they condemned those who violated international law and committed acts of aggression. Although neither mentioned the United States, it was clear to all whom those leaders had foremost in mind.

It then took three weeks of intense behind-the-scenes diplomacy before the Bush administration scored a vital victory. On October 16, 2003, the UN Security Council unanimously passed Resolution 1511, which acknowledged the American occupation and called for a multilateral force to eventually take over. In doing so, the Security Council handed the Bush administration a legal fig leaf to cover what many experts, including Kofi Annan, condemned as a naked war of imperialism in Iraq.[7]

An essential ingredient for Iraq's rebuilding would be to reduce its foreign debt. Iraq owed $116 billion in loans and another $100 billion in reparations to Kuwait. Of the loans, Iraq was in debt for $45.5 billion to Middle East countries, $41.5 billion to the eighteen members of the Paris Club of democratic industrialized countries, $8 billion to Russia, $5 billion to China, and $4 billion to other countries.

Secretary of State Powell convened an international conference of twenty-five potential donors to Iraq at Madrid on October 23 and 24, 2003. In all, $33 billion was pledged, with more than half ($18.4 billion) promised by the United States, $5 billion from Japan, $812 million from the European Union, $500 million from Kuwait, and far smaller grants from most of the other participants. The IMF and World Bank, respectively, promised $9.2 billion and $5.5 billion in low-interest loans.

The follow-through was not as swift. Although the U.S. Treasury signed a check for America's full pledge the following month, few other pledges would be fulfilled. New horror stories of the rampant corruption and waste of the American-led reconstruction caused many governments to have second thoughts about the wisdom and ethics of handing over money to the Bush administration, which would then determine its distribution.

Bush appointed James Baker, his father's secretary of state, to lead the effort with the Paris Club of major international banks involved in development. Once again the results fell short of hopes. The Paris Club debated the issue but failed to reach a specific number. Baker then tried to talk Iraq's fellow Arab states to write off that vast debt. He received nothing but polite promises to consider the matter. It took another a year of hard bargaining until, in November 2004, the Paris Club agreed to cancel $33 billion of Iraq's debt.[8]

Most preferred to work through the United Nations and other international aid organizations. The most important of these was the International Reconstruction Fund for Iraq (IRFI), which was jointly managed by the United Nations Development Group and World Bank. As of June 30, 2006, the fund had received $1.5 billion in donations from twenty-six countries.

Hard as it was to collect donations for such an unpopular war, it was even more challenging actually to disburse the money. The worsening insurgency and civil war either destroyed projects or put them on hold. By December 30, 2005, IRFI had expended only $900 million. And the problems, sadly, did not end there. UN aid was channeled directly into the coffers of the Iraq government, a financial black hole as opaque as that of the Bush administration's program, although far less voracious.

13

That Elusive "Smoking Gun"

While the Bush team was compelled to ask the international community for money, it initially drew the line at enlisting expertise that could have saved them time, money, and, above all, credibility. The president spurned an offer by Hans Blix and Mohamed ElBaradei to bring their inspection teams back to Iraq to help the hunt for WMDs. Once again ideological correctness trumped American national interests.

The conservatives had an enormous credibility gap, not just with Iraq but over virtually all issues and with virtually all countries. At the top of the conservative list of reasons for invading Iraq was to find that "proof—the smoking gun" before it came "in the form of a mushroom cloud." It was widely believed that the Bush team would plant weapons to justify its war against Iraq. The president chose not to diminish that not unreasonable fear by not letting UN inspectors do their job.

The question then for the White House was which American organization was capable of fulfilling that mission. To the administration's chagrin, the answer was none. So it was decided to strip an artillery battalion of its cannons, designate it the Iraq Survey Group, add CIA officers and other experts, and hand it a list of 946 suspected sites to search.

The fourteen hundred personnel of the Iraq Survey Group spent nearly two years and $1 billion inspecting the listed WMD sites as well as scores of others, and interrogating thousands of officials, scientists, and technicians. They found nothing but the debris of former programs and heard a consistent story that the weapons had been destroyed. On January 26, 2004, David Kay, the inspection chief, admitted before the Senate Armed Services Committee that "it turns out we were all wrong. . . . Why could we all be so wrong?"[1]

The answer is crystal clear—President Bush and his fellow conservatives were able to impose their ideological zeal and blindness on most other Americans and smear as unpatriotic the realists who dismissed the notion of an Iraqi threat to the United States and who warned that an invasion of Iraq would be an utter disaster for American national power, wealth, and honor. Scott Ritter condemned the Bush administration for a "rush to war" that "ignored our advice and the body of factual data we used, and instead relied on rumor, speculation, exaggeration, and falsification to mislead the American people and their elected representatives into supporting a war that is rapidly turning into a quagmire. We knew the truth about Iraq's WMD. Sadly no one listened." Hans Blix explained that "like the former days of the witch hunt, they were convinced that [the WMDs] exist." By putting ideological zealotry first, the conservatives had actually "bred a lot of terrorism and a lot of hatred to the western world." The UN inspections alone cost $80 million a year and were essential to containing Iraq. Bush's war had so far cost America $166 billion for the first eighteen months alone and provoked worsening terrorism across Iraq and elsewhere around the world. Which was the most cost-effective policy?[2]

If the reason for that conservative obsession is relatively easy to expose, the solution to another puzzle is a bit murkier. Why would Saddam refuse to reveal to the world that he had no such weapons and thus end more than a decade of crippling economic sanctions and military strikes and, ultimately, prevent an American invasion? It comes down to deterrence. The Middle East is a very tough neighborhood. Saddam feared that if his enemies, especially the Iranians, knew he had no WMDs, they might be more likely to attack Iraq. He also apparently believed that the American buildup was just a bluff and that the Bush administration would not be crazy enough to actually invade Iraq. In that he surely miscalculated.[3]

As for the alleged alliance between Iraq and Al Qaeda, nothing was found. Nonetheless, the conservatives continued to link Saddam and bin Laden. On May 1, 2003, President Bush declared that the "liberation of Iraq is a crucial advance in the campaign against terror. We've removed an ally of al Qaeda."[4]

14

Imposing Democracy

In their war on terrorism and tyranny, President Bush and his fellow conservatives declared democracy to be their most important weapon. The transformation of Iraq into a democratic showcase would ignite a domino effect of democratic revolutions across the Middle East and beyond, thus eliminating terrorism and tyranny. The conservative crusade in Iraq may have been a cause for widespread violent upheavals across the Middle East in 2011, but so far no liberal democracies have emerged. Bush explained that "the failure of Iraqi democracy would embolden terrorists around the world, increase dangers to the American people, and extinguish the hopes of millions in the region. Iraqi democracy will succeed, and that success will send forth the news from Damascus to Tehran, that freedom can be the future of every nation."[1] It was that simple.

Iraq's democratic revolution was imposed in a series of stages, each of which was preceded by vigorous debate in the White House and Coalition Provisional Authority (CPA) over how fast and how far to go. The first step came on July 13, 2003, when the CPA set up the Iraq Governing Council of twenty-five members who represented the spectrum of Iraq's leading political and religious groups, including thirteen Arab Sunnis, five Arab Shiites, five Kurds, a Christian, and a Turk; three were women. The Council's role was to advise the Americans and oversee a future constitutional convention, war crimes trials, and elections.

The White House scheduled Iraq's first democratic elections for June 30, 2004, and asked the United Nations to supervise them. To investigate the feasibility of that date, Secretary-General Annan dispatched a mission to Iraq from February 6 to 13. On February 24 Annan announced the mission's conclusions: no elections for Iraq were conceivable before the end of 2004 or early 2005. Fair elections would require at least four trained people at each of the thirty thousand polling stations; it would take months to train and mobilize those workers. And then there was the question of security. Without an Iraqi army or police force and with American troops stretched thin to the snapping point, who would protect the millions of people lined up waiting to vote from terrorist bombs and guns? That news enraged the conservatives who wanted Iraqi elections before the November 2004 presidential election in the United States.

If elections were not feasible before that date, perhaps a formal return of Iraqi sovereignty was. The White House handpicked an interim Iraqi government with Ayad Allawi, a Shiite Arab with years of ties with the CIA and State Department, as the prime minister, and Ghazi Ajil al-Yawar, a Sunni Arab, in the ceremonial post of president. On June 28, 2004, the United States officially transferred power to the Allawi government.

This move terminated the CPA. Henceforth the United States would manage Iraq indirectly through its embassy. John Negroponte, a career diplomat with four decades of experience, became the ambassador. He stood alongside Paul Bremer as power was symbolically handed back to the Iraqis.

The new government's most important task was to prepare Iraq for National Assembly elections, which would be held on January 31, 2005, and the drafting and implementation of a constitution later that year. The elections for the 275-member National Assembly took place as scheduled. Shiite Islamist parties won 140 seats, the Kurdish bloc took 75 seats, and a range of other groups and candidates picked up the rest. Few Sunnis were elected, since their leaders had urged their people to boycott the elections.

In all, the elections were a great victory for the Shiite version of radical Islamism, with a core of adherents holding a plurality of 128 seats. The ultimate winner was Iran, which covertly aided most of the Shiite parties and politicians. Yet that ideological unity could not easily paper over the ancient antagonisms among the tribes and clans that won seats in the National Assembly. It would take another two months of haggling before a fragile coalition emerged to form a government.[2]

All along, the Bush team gave the Iraqis some curious lessons in democracy. In March Ibrahim al-Jaafari appeared to be gaining the edge over Allawi, Washington's candidate. The White House tried to pressure the Iraqis not to pick al-Jaafari, arguing that he was too close to the Islamists, especially Moktada al-Sadr, the radical anti-American cleric and leader of the Mahdi Army, the largest militia. This ham-fisted tactic backfired. On April 7, 2005, al-Jaafari became the prime minister.

The contradiction between the Bush team's declared vision of imposing a democracy upon Iraq and determination to control the results could not stay out of the spotlight. Word leaked that the Defense Department was planting favorable news stories in Iraq's mass media by bribing reporters. This created a glaring credibility gap for the reporters and their newspapers or television stations. The White House actually downplayed the scandal, claiming there was nothing wrong with this kind of manipulation. Regardless, the effect was to discredit that "fourth branch" of government, so crucial to any democracy.[3]

Al-Jaafari lasted little more than a year. Sunnis and Kurds complained bitterly that the prime minister and his cabinet were abusing their powers and forging closer ties with Iran. The White House brokered a deal by which al-Jaafari resigned and Nuri Kamal al-Maliki formed a government on May 28, 2006. Al-Maliki had the advantage of being supported by Ayatollah Ali al-Sistani, Abdul Aziz al-Hakim, who led the Supreme Council of the Islamic Revolution, and al-Sadr. With this Islamist backing, it was no surprise that the Sunnis and Kurds were soon hurling the same accusations against al-Maliki that they had against al-Jaafari.

A constitution was eventually hammered out and ratified by parliament on October 15, 2005. Under the constitution, Iraq's government was declared Islamic, democratic, and federal. On that, virtually everyone agreed. The devil as always was in the details, where political compromises eventually capped prolonged periods of haggling. The result was a political system with a relatively weak national government and significant powers devolved to regions, ethnic groups, and religious sects.

Iraq's second national election was held on March 7, 2010. International observers lauded that election for its minimal violence and voter fraud. Allawi's Iraqiya Party won a plurality with 91 seats in the 325-seat parliament, followed by al-Maliki's State of Law Coalition with 89, al-Sadr's Iraqi National Alliance with 70, and the Kurdish Alliance with 43. Although Allawi was secular and pro-American, the results revealed that Iraq as a whole remained sharply tilted toward Islamism, Iran, and anti-Americanism, with the combined seats of al-Maliki and al-Sadr reaching 159. Both men swore they would resist Allawi's attempts to form a government. Paradoxically, even a seeming success in Iraq almost invariably had its negative side. The state-building policy faced two dilemmas. First, the efforts to create a Western-style liberal democracy exacerbated sectarian tensions and led to ethnic cleansing and civil war. Second, the majority Shiite population was largely pro-Iranian and anti-American, and thus prevented the stable power balance between Iraq and Iran promoted by Washington's containment policies from 1990 to 2003. Finally, regardless of who formed a government, the winners would preside over a shattered economy, mass poverty, and joblessness, with nearly two million displaced people in the country and another two million refugees in other countries.

Nonetheless, to date the Bush administration's democratic revolution from above on has been a limited success in Iraq. The country today does have such democratic trappings as mass elections, representative government, and constitutional rights. Yet there is often an unbridgeable gap between the appearance and substance of democracy. Democracies are illiberal if their constitutions, elections, legislatures, and other institutions are not rooted in a liberal culture. As for the essence of democracy, it may take generations before Iraqis internalize a democratic political culture.

15

The Spoils of War

The immediate beneficiaries of the Iraq War were the corporations that won contracts to operate there. Not surprisingly, the Bush team at first allowed only American firms to bid on the contracts and rewarded only those that were heavy contributors to the Republican Party such as Halliburton and then-subsidiary Kellogg Brown & Root (KBR), Bechtel, Fluor, Parsons Corporation, Washington Group International, Louis Berger Group, Foster Wheeler, Schlumberger, ExxonMobil, and Chevron.

It was payback time, to the tune of tens of billions of dollars in contracts ladled out in no-bids, rigged-bids, or limited bids for corporations that had handed tens of millions of dollars to George W. Bush and his fellow Republicans. American firms without close Republican ties often received only a few days' notice before a bid's deadline or no notice at all. In all, during George W. Bush's eight years in power, the amount of federal contracts to the private sector doubled from $207 billion in 2000 to $500 billion in 2008, about half of which were no-bid contracts.[1]

The Bush administration even excluded British companies from any primary contracts; they and other foreign firms were only allowed subcontracts. If the conservatives cut Britain out of the spoils with a shrug, they gleefully slammed the door in the face of the companies from other countries. On December 10, 2003, the White House pointedly declared that France, Germany, and Russia would be barred from $18.5 billion of new contracts. However, the following day Bush performed his latest flip-flop when he had to ask all three of those countries to lower the debt Iraq owned them. The complaints of America's allies and the White House's need for cooperation from other countries and institutions finally provoked a grudging shift in policy. On February 12, 2004, the White House announced that it would open $6 billion in prime contracts to all countries that had supported America's occupation.[2]

Those that won bids were selected in a secret process approved by Secretary of Defense Rumsfeld and his under secretary Douglas Feith. The political payback was as utterly shameless as it was blatant. In May 2003 Joe Allbaugh, Bush's former presidential campaign manager and then director of the Federal Emergency Management Agency (FEMA), along with Edward Rogers and Lanny Griffith, assistants to Bush's father, set up the New Bridge Strategies Company to guide potential contractors to lucrative contracts. Not surprisingly, Halliburton, which Dick Cheney had headed from 1995 to 2000, won most of the first year's 220 projects, worth $10.5 billion. Lewis Libby, Cheney's chief of staff, approved many of the deals. Nonetheless, Cheney publicly declared, "I have absolutely no influence, involvement, knowledge of in any way, shape, or form of contracts led by the Corps of Engineers or anybody else in the federal government." He also claimed that "I have no financial interest in Halliburton of any kind and haven't had any for over three years." In reality, Cheney still owned 433,333 stock options and received $150,000 a year in deferred payments.[3]

If ethical people were enraged by how Halliburton got its $35 billion worth of contracts to date, they became even more incensed when they learned what Halliburton did with these contracts. Halliburton blatantly overcharged American taxpayers for such services as supplying meals for the troops and gasoline for their vehicles; the price gouging for fuel alone was $250 million. Nonetheless, the Pentagon not only did not prosecute Halliburton for fraud, but paid every penny claimed.

This was just the tip of the corruption iceberg. A 2006 government audit of $25 billion of contracts found endemic corruption, favoritism, graft, and incompetence, with only a small portion of the projects actually completed. By a cautious estimate, the waste, fraud, and abuse were at least $10 billion. The Pentagon identified as "questionable" $3.2 billion of $20 billion in contracts for KBR and $1.4 billion in "unreasonable" overcharges for Halliburton itself. And the corruption did not just enrich fat-cat contributors to the Republican Party. The contractors were actually helping to finance the insurgency by handing over hundreds of millions of dollars in protection money. Overhead costs alone devoured more than half of all expenditures. And most projects never even left the drawing boards. Billions of dollars have been annually funneled from America's taxpayers to corporations that supplied nothing more than blueprints! The most blatant theft to date was $8.8 billion in cash that the Federal Reserve sent to Baghdad in 2003 to jumpstart the Iraqi government that the Americans were trying to devise—all $8.8 billion disappeared down the Iraqi rabbit hole. American inspector generals have searched in vain for it ever since.[4]

The corruption was hardly confined to Americans. Hundreds of Iraqi exiles descended on the country, many with a get-rich-and-powerful-quick mentality. Ahmed Chalabi was the most notorious carpetbagger. To the Bush team's embarrassment, among the few looters nabbed by American troops were some of the six hundred men of the so-called Free Iraqi Forces that INC chair Ahmad Chalabi brought back with him. Alas, this was just the beginning of Chalabi's looting—he took carpetbagging to obscene heights of abuse. But Chalabi's worst betrayal was when he told the Iranian government that the CIA had cracked their code. They promptly changed it and thus deprived the United States of vital intelligence. In response to the subsequent CIA outrage, the Bush team began to back away from their "hero." But, rather than arrest Chalabi—or at the very least banish him from Iraq—their only "punishment" was to cancel his monthly check for $355,000, courtesy of American taxpayers via the Pentagon. The Bush team's subsidy to Chalabi was but a drop in an ocean of American wealth squandered and looted as a result of the conservative crusade in Iraq.[5]

Tragically the abuses did not end with the toleration of corruption on a mind-boggling scale. This corruption was exacerbated by the Bush administration's policy of shutting out Iraqi firms from the contract process even though they offered bids at a fraction—sometimes one-tenth—of those of American contractors for the same type of work. The usual excuse was that the Iraqi contractors were not qualified. In reality, most were far more competent and efficient in understanding the work and getting it done. After all, Iraq had achieved significant economic development before Saddam squandered it through two disastrous wars and the resulting international sanctions. It was mostly Iraqi companies that had developed their country's economic infrastructure and industries.

As usual, real reasons underlay the official justifications. The White House rejected Iraqi bids on ideological and political grounds: most of the Iraqi contractors were state-owned, and none had apparently contributed to the Republican Party.

However, eventually work did trickle down to the Iraqi companies via subcontracts from the American corporations. Yet this policy stunted and distorted Iraq's development in several ways. Iraqi companies remained dependent on, and thus subservient to, America's corporate giants. Most of the money was either siphoned off to swell the bank accounts of insiders or eaten up by layers of overhead bureaucracy, and thus little trickled down into the Iraqi economy.[6]

In all, the way the Bush administration ladled out Iraq construction money was the perfect storm of creed and greed. Conservatives claim that the private sector always outperforms the public sector. And it was the perfect way to reward the heavy contributors to the Republican Party.

Self-regulation of the private sector is among the more sacred of conservative shibboleths and has proven to be as much a chimera in Iraq as anywhere else. The contractors were a law onto themselves and most of them appeared to take full advantage of that. The Bush administration gave contractors immunity from prosecution in Iraqi courts and forced the Iraqi government to continue that practice after it officially took over on June 28, 2004. Even when abuses were discovered, it was virtually impossible to recover the lost funds, let alone fire or prosecute the contractors.

Magnifying the corruption and incompetence was the degree to which the Bush team privatized its war. The numbers were staggering. In all, the federal government paid private contractors $100 billion for an array of purposes in Iraq from 2003 until 2008. The numbers peaked in July 2007, when 182,000 people worked in Iraq as American contractors or subcontractors, of which 21,000 were Americans, 118,000 were Iraqis, and 43,000 were from other countries. The number of private contract employees rose steadily until by February 2008, there were 196,000 contractors in Iraq and Afghanistan, more than the 182,000 American troops in both countries. No corporation employed more than KBR, which at its peak had more than 54,000 workers in Iraq doing an array of jobs such as driving trucks, cooking meals, and washing clothes for the troops, and delivering mail. Iraqi firms employing Iraqi citizens could have performed all of those jobs at a fraction of the cost.[7]

The Bush administration hired private contractors not just to reconstruct Iraq but to provide security. From 2004 to 2008, $12 billion was spent on the services of private security firms. That private security peaked in 2006 when 181 firms supplied forty-eight thousand personnel, some with monthly salaries as high as $33,000![8]

So how did the "magic of the marketplace" perform in Iraq? A harsh reality belied the conservative dogma that the private sector outperforms the public sector while imposing less of a burden on taxpayers. An August 2008 Congressional Budget Office study found that there was no cost difference between using American troops or mercenaries, though the former are much easier to control than the latter.[9]

The private security contractors were not bound by the same rules of engagement as the military. The result was a Darwinian world where each firm got away with whatever it could. Blackwater was the largest recipient of these security contracts and the loosest cannon among the private security firms. Critics accused Blackwater employees of behaving like unlawful combatants by firing, and killing, indiscriminately at traffic jams that blocked their way or at anyone who appeared suspicious. The most notorious incident occurred on September 16, 2007, when five Blackwater security people opened fire at a traffic circle crammed with cars in Baghdad. There was no evidence to back the Blackwater claim that they had been fired upon. The employees eventually went on trial for the murder of seventeen Iraqis, but a federal court, packed with conservative judges, threw out the case.

However lucrative the landing of an Iraq contract may have been, it did have its drawbacks, especially for those who worked in the field. By December 31, 2007, 1,123 civilian contractors had been killed.[10] The worsening death toll and criticism caused corporate giants to take their profits and run. Bechtel announced on November 9, 2004, that it would withdraw from Iraq on November 26, 2006. This ended an intense three-year involvement in Iraq during which it pocketed $2.3 billion in taxpayer dollars, suffered the deaths of fifty-two employees, and endured persistent congressional and public criticism of its operations for being blatantly corrupt and inept. Halliburton disinvested itself of KBR on April 5, 2007.

Not that the public sector was any less incompetent or dishonest when it was in charge. In 2004 and 2005 alone, the Pentagon lost track of 190,000 firearms that it was supposed to supply the Iraqi army and police force that it was trying to build. Not only private contractors made off like bandits. Army and air force engineers overcharged taxpayers for shoddy, delayed, or nonexistent work.[11]

The corruption's scale and range was so outrageous that a few Democrats actually dared to speak out. Sen. Christopher Dodd explained that the Bush team "believes that they can get away with it; that the Congress will not do anything about it."[12]

Indeed, in that at least the Bush administration was prescient. There were no congressional investigations or special prosecutors, let alone impeachment of officials, for committing such blatant multi-million- and even multi-billion-dollar crime sprees. To date no one either in the Bush administration or the corporations has ever been indicted, let alone convicted, of corruption.

The reason was simple. The party that had mercilessly tried to destroy President Clinton for his failed Whitewater deal a dozen years before he entered the White House, his adultery, and other alleged sins now completely dominated all three branches of the federal government and had intimidated the mass media into being the political lapdog, rather than the guard dog, of democracy. And then, after the Democrats retook Congress following the November 2006 elections, they were too emasculated to launch any serious investigations of alleged "high crimes and misdemeanors" of the Bush administration.

All of this private and public American corruption and ineptness did not set a particularly good example for the Iraqi leaders and people upon whom the Bush administration was trying to impose a liberal democracy.

ROUND THREE:
CATACLYSMS

"I don't want to read in the *New York Times* that we are facing an insurgency. I don't want anyone in the cabinet to say it is an insurgency. I don't think we are there yet."
—GEORGE W. BUSH

"We will accept nothing less than complete and final victory."
—GEORGE W. BUSH

"What the president says in effect is we've got to press on in honor of the memory of those who have fallen. Another way to say that is we've got to have more men fall to honor the memory of those who have already fallen."
—RICHARD ARMITAGE

"Let me say this as plainly as I can. By August 31, 2010, our combat mission in Iraq will end."
—PRESIDENT BARACK OBAMA

16

"Bring 'Em On!"

An insurgency in Iraq was all but inevitable. Saddam Hussein knew that the Iraqi army could not stave off the American onslaught.[1] To stand and fight would play into the enemy's hands. So instead, he prepared for a guerrilla war against the invaders by placing arsenals packed with guns, explosives, and money in strategic spots across the country. He even had the book *Black Hawk Down*, Mark Bowden's riveting account of the October 2003 battle between Somali insurgents and American forces, translated and distributed to his commanders. This strategy was to grind down the Americans with an escalating insurgency until they finally quit the county in a humiliating defeat, much like the Soviets in Afghanistan.

Yet the insurgency's growth and virulence was magnified by four key Bush administration decisions. The first was to deploy only about one-third the number of troops deemed by experts necessary to pacify the country. The occupation was initially composed of 139,000 American, 11,000 British, and 10,000 troops from seventeen junior partners. A year after the invasion, the United States and Britain had reduced their troops to 110,000 and 8,200, respectively; although the number of other countries contributing troops rose to twenty-six, each contributed no more than token amounts. So overall, the number of allied troops fell as the number of bombings and shootings increased.

The Bush team compounded that initial blunder with the decisions in May 2003 to eliminate Iraqi security forces and the Ba'ath Party. This not only destroyed the two major pillars of stability in the country, but also turned those hundreds of thousands of now unemployed soldiers and officials into enemies of the occupation.

Finally, the "search, destroy, and withdraw" strategy chosen to quell the insurgency instead exacerbated it. Surrounding a neighborhood or village with troops who would then systematically kick in doors, shoot anyone who appeared threatening, ransack homes for weapons, and drag away young men for harsh interrogations and prison were at once tactical successes and strategic failures. While those operations killed or captured thousands of insurgents, they also killed or captured countless innocent bystanders or destroyed their homes and livelihoods. This destruction converted wary political fence-sitters into enraged rebels determined to avenge their ruined lives and honor.

As if those blunders were not egregious enough, they were spiced with far right-wing bluster. Lt. Gen. Ricardo Sanchez, the American ground commander, articulated in July 2003 the conservative "flypaper theory" of counterterrorism by which Iraq would become, as he put it, "a terrorist magnet" that would "prevent the American people from having to go through with attacks back in the United States." When asked his reaction to the growing number of insurgent attacks, President Bush brayed "Bring 'em on!"[2]

Thus did the president and the general enthusiastically express a "strategy" that essentially used American troops and civilians, as well as other foreign troops, aid workers, and the Iraqi people as decoys or bait for terrorism. Yet few people seemed to notice, let alone care. The "shock and awe" of the media blitz by which the Bush team had marketed its war had not yet worn off for most Americans.

The insurgents were happy to comply with what was a godsend for America's enemies everywhere. The war in Iraq spawned ever more anti-American hatred and recruits for terrorist groups, while Islamist and other terrorist attacks increased worldwide since the March 2003 invasion. Iraq did indeed become a magnet for hate-filled Islamists from around the world who were eager for a chance to kill Americans. They slipped in by the hundreds and inflicted enormous death and destruction across the country, even though they probably never numbered more than five percent of all the insurgents.[3]

One of the greatest ironies of the conservative crusade in Iraq was that Al Qaeda had been an enemy of Saddam and had no operational presence there before the American invasion. It was not until early 2004 that a group that called itself Al Qaeda in Iraq, under the Jordanian Abu Musaab al-Zarqawi, opened a very deadly business there. Al-Zarqawi had previously led the group Ansar al-Islam, which fought against the Kurds in northern Iraq. After American and Kurdish forces routed Ansar al-Islam, al-Zarqawi and his followers slipped back into Iraq from Syria with a new name for themselves.

Yet Al Qaeda did not monopolize the foreign Sunni fighters in Iraq. Many of them fought in their own small groups or joined local Sunni militias. Al Qaeda became a convenient label for the coalition forces to put on any foreign fighters they killed or captured who may have been carrying Al Qaeda pamphlets or a laptop that had accessed Al Qaeda websites. As a result, Al Qaeda's numbers may have been grossly exaggerated.

The backgrounds of the foreign fighters were diverse but most came from the Middle East. Of 135 foreign fighters in custody by July 2007, Saudis made up 45 percent, Syrians and Lebanese 15 percent, and North Africans 10 percent; about half of the Saudis came to act as suicide bombers.[4]

Foreign fighters actually began arriving in Iraq before the invasion, but they hardly received the red carpet treatment. Saddam feared that many were Sunni or Shiite Islamists who might eventually turn their guns against him. Writing in August 2003, terrorist expert Jessica Stern explained that "in the run-up to the war, most Iraqis viewed the foreign volunteers who were rushing in to fight against America as trouble-makers, and Saddam Hussein's forces killed many of them. Today . . . these foreigners are increasingly welcomed by the public, especially in the former Baathist strongholds north of Baghdad."[5]

Many Sunni fighters passed through Syria. While Damascus has at times cooperated with the United States by providing intelligence and interrogating suspects, it has also turned a blind eye to the transit or refuge of Al Qaeda operatives. Many of Al Qaeda in Iraq's recruits, arms, and money arrived via Syria. By some accounts Syria's involvement was at times more than passive. Before the American invasion, Damascus outright coordinated the flow "between cells in Europe and Ansar al-Islam training camps in

northern Iraq."[6] The foreign fighters were certainly more deadly and destructive than the Ba'athists, who also numbered about one in twenty insurgents. Apparently Saddam's preparations for a guerrilla war did not
extend beyond setting up arms caches. There was no master plan for resistance, just an order to kill as many invaders as possible. During his decades
in power Saddam had so brutally cowed any real or imagined rivals to his
rule that few among his Ba'ath Party cadres or his officer corps dared take
the initiative. Saddam had little operational control over his security forces
before the bombs and missiles began dropping on March 19 and none after
he literally went underground.

Nonetheless, the systematic killing or capture of the Ba'athist leadership
steadily undercut the morale and prowess of the Ba'athist insurgents.
Eventually all fifty-five of the top Ba'athist leaders were eliminated. The most
spectacular operation occurred on July 22, when a tip-off led to an assault
on a mansion in Mosul where Saddam's sons Uday and Qusay Hussein were
hiding. The two were killed in the shootout, and the informant pocketed a
$35 million award. Saddam Hussein, however, remained at large for nine
months after the invasion and occasionally forwarded tapes to the mass
media calling on Iraqis to rise up against the Americans. Then, on December
13, 2003, the Americans nabbed the dictator himself—filthy, disoriented,
and cowering alone in a bunker.

Nine of ten insurgents were Iraqis for whom neither Islamism nor
Ba'athism was their primary inspiration. At its height, the insurgency consisted of hundreds of groups with varying numbers of fighters. They did
not confine venting their rage on the invaders in their midst. Many of the
groups hated and killed each other just as zealously. The insurgent groups
were split along religious, ethnic, and tribal lines that often overlapped.
Tribal rather than ethnic or even religious ties proved to be the most powerful motivation for most insurgents. Three of four Iraqis were members of
one of around 150 tribes. Although most tribes have only one religious or
ethnic identity, some are mixed.[7]

Exaggerated notions of honor characterize tribal societies. Vengeance for
perceived or genuine insults is essential for restoring honor. Justice demands
at least an eye for an eye and is inflicted not by an impartial judicial system
but by the aggrieved as well. Thus tribal societies are plagued by feuds of

spiraling hatred and retribution. While the participants may weary of the endless violence and fear, honor demands that they not stop until they get in the last blow. Feuds only end when a respected and neutral third party can arrange a face-saving halt to the cycle of murder and mayhem, often with the payment of blood money as restitution.

Vengeance was only one motive. Most of those who fought had literally little or nothing left to lose. Mired in poverty, violence, and devastation, with no prospects of a job or marriage, young men flocked to the insurgent groups that gave them pay, guns, and purpose.

The insurgents did not just target Americans, but singled out for murder anyone who collaborated with the occupiers, such as Iraqi officials, police, and soldiers. Their victims did not end there. They also murdered members of the professional class who might benefit from the new regime, such as doctors, lawyers, and managers. Finally the Sunnis and Shiites began indiscriminately slaughtering each other.

The insurgents understood that their ranks would swell with the misery of the population. To that end they sought to spread chaos and anti-American hatred by destroying economic infrastructure by blowing up electrical power stations, oil pipelines, sewage treatment facilities, and water purification plants. They also attacked the humanitarian and development projects of the international governmental organizations (IGOs) and nongovernmental organizations (NGOs), and did not hesitate to murder their personnel.

Initially most of the insurgents were Sunni Arabs. The reason was clear enough: they stood to lose the most from the war. Although they numbered only about 20 percent of the population, the Sunni Arabs under Saddam had brutally dominated and exploited the Shiites and Kurds. It would be a very harsh payback time if the Americans set up a parliament with free elections and proportional representation.

For the first few years of the insurgency, most Shiites sat on the sidelines. The Americans were doing their dirty work for them by fighting the mostly Sunni rebels and setting up a government that the Shiites would dominate. Ali al-Sistani, the grand ayatollah for Iraqi Shiites, continually called on his people to cooperate with the Americans.

Al-Sistani had enormous influence over the Badr Corps, the second largest Shiite militia. The Badr Corps was the military wing of the Supreme

Islamic Iraqi Council (SIIC), previously known as the Supreme Council for the Islamic Revolution in Iraq (SCIRI), with its spiritual and political head-quarters in Karbala. It was founded in 1982 during the Iraq-Iran War under Tehran's mentorship to rally Iraqi Shiites against Saddam's regime. Like Hezbollah and Hamas, SIIC was a broad political revolutionary movement that at times wielded terrorism as one of an array of tactics to advance al-Sistani's goals. It did not openly fight against the American occupation but instead focused on mobilizing the Shiite population by promoting recon-struction and development projects, all the while stockpiling arms.

Of all the Shiite groups, the worst potential enemy the United States faced in Iraq was Moktada al-Sadr's Mahdi Army, which numbered as many as 50,000 armed men in Sadr City, a Baghdad slum packed with over a million people. The Mahdi Army had ties with Iran's Quds Force and Hezbollah, from which it received training, equipment, weapons, and bombs, along with instructions on how to organize a popular movement that mobilized support by solving local economic and social problems.

Al-Sadr was the son of a prominent Shiite cleric who was assassinated in 1999. Although he lacked his father's theological depth and gravitas, he nonetheless inherited the central mosque and his father's authority over Sadr City. Al-Sadr is vehemently anti-American. Frequent skirmishes broke out between his militia and the American forces.

The Americans faced a dilemma with al-Sadr. If they tolerated him, his authority and militia would grow more powerful. If they fought against him, they would need tens of thousands of troops and months of time to fight their way through Sadr City. While they would undoubtedly kill or capture thousands of militiamen, they would drive many more times that number of survivors into the Mahdi Army's ranks. Decapitation posed its own chal-lenge. The coalition issued a warrant for al-Sadr and eleven of his top ad-visers in August 2003, but they went into hiding, most likely in Iran. Ayatollah al-Sistani was able to cut a cease-fire deal with al-Sadr.

Eventually the Shiites did join the killing, but mostly against Sunnis. The catalyst was al-Zarqawi, who sought to provoke a three-way war among the Sunnis, Shiites, and the coalition forces by setting off bombs in Shiite neigh-borhoods and mosques. Thus did a civil war mesh with the insurgency, as Sunni and Shiite militias increasingly turned their guns and bombs on each other. Villages and neighborhoods in which the sects once lived and worked side by side were eventually "cleansed" by the more powerful group. As if the interrelated insurgency and civil war were not complex enough, many of the killings were committed by criminal gangs that also mushroomed and ran rampant.

17

Abu Ghraib, Hearts, and Minds

For three years after the invasion, virtually everything the Bush team did in Iraq fed rather than starved the insurgency. Indeed, the Bush administration's policies provided a textbook example of how not to fight rebels.

Self-deception was the worst impediment to implementing a comprehensive counterinsurgency strategy. In the face of the worsening insurgency and civil war, President Bush and other conservatives in and beyond the White House issued ever terser statements claiming that everything was under control. They denied that Iraq was engulfed by an ever more vicious insurgency and civil war. Typical was the exchange between Rob Richer, the CIA Near East Division chief, and Defense Secretary Rumsfeld during an NSC meeting on November 11, 2003, described in Bob Woodward's book *State of Denial*. After Richer stated that the CIA was "'seeing the establishment of an insurgency in Iraq.' . . . . Rumsfeld cut him off. 'That's a strong word. What do you mean? How do you define insurgency?' Rumsfeld dismissed that reality even after Richer defined and systematically applied the concept to Iraq. President Bush then echoed the defense secretary's wishful thinking: 'I don't want to read in The *New York Times* that we are facing an insurgency. I don't want anyone in the cabinet to say it is an insurgency. I don't think we are there yet.'"[1]

Among the traps in which the Bush administration conservatives snared themselves was the same "body count" obsession that so deluded their

Vietnam War counterparts. They became fixated on how many insurgents were being killed or captured.

Gen. Peter Pace, the chairman of the Joint Chiefs of Staff, tried to disabuse them of this delusion during an NSC meeting on April 9, 2004: "The most important military strategy is to accelerate the governance track. You can kill folks for the next 27 years and you're not going to have a better environment. What you have to do is provide enough security inside of which governance can take place, and that's why governance is so important, they're intertwined."[2]

Richard Armitage, the deputy secretary of state, captured the conservative mind-set: "What the president says in effect is we've got to press on in honor of those who have fallen. Another way to say that is we've got to have more men fall to honor those who have already fallen."[3]

Like the White House, most of the Pentagon's top brass did not understand the nature of the war they were fighting in Iraq. Generals John Abizaid and Ricardo Sanchez, who respectively headed Central Command and led coalition ground forces, had no experience fighting insurgents. War for them was about imposing massive numbers of troops and firepower to pulverize an enemy and intimidate any survivors.

These "search, destroy, and withdraw" tactics only played into the hands of the insurgents by feeding the vicious cycle of violence, destruction, despair, and hatred. Thus did the Americans face in Iraq the same "hydra dilemma" they had provoked in Vietnam. No matter how many guerrillas they killed, others soon filled the ranks.

The worst instance came after a mob murdered four Blackwater employees in Fallujah on March 31, 2004. This prompted the Pentagon to launch a military operation that eventually flattened much of Fallujah and killed or drove off many of its 250,000 inhabitants. So much for hearts and minds.

The Americans desperately tried to rebuild the Iraqi army that they had abolished, along with a national police force. The guerrillas infiltrated the ranks of the army and police to gather intelligence, ruin morale, and stir rebellion.[4]

Intelligence is essential to any successful counterinsurgency strategy. As the CIA explained repeatedly to the White House, the abolition of Iraq's intelligence agency, the Mukhabarat, hobbled America's counterinsurgency struggle in Iraq. In September 2003 Director Tenet formally proposed that the CIA create and control an Iraqi intelligence agency. Ideological and bureaucratic politics blocked that proposal until July 2004 when the White House finally gave Langley the green light.[5]

Perhaps the worst blow to American efforts to quell the worsening insurgency were the revelations of the gratuitous abuse of prisoners. Once again the Bush team sacrificed law and civilized behavior on the altar of conservative "might makes right" bullying, sadism, and vengeance.

Tragically, the most enduring images of the Bush administration's "war on terror" may be an American soldier dragging a naked Iraqi prisoner by a leash, or a hooded figure with electrodes attached to his body and with his arms outstretched as if he awaited crucifixion. These disturbing photos are only two of thousands documenting the American abuse of prisoners. Although the Abu Ghraib prison near Baghdad became notorious, thousands of prisoners were humiliated and tortured at thirteen other sites in Iraq and at dozens of others around the world.[6]

The horrific abuses at Abu Ghraib were first uncovered in October 2003 during a inspection by the Red Cross. Its report reached the disturbing conclusion that "methods of physical and psychological coercion used by the interrogators appeared to be part of the standard operating procedure by military intelligence personnel to obtain confessions and extract information."[7] That report was kept secret. In return for access, the Red Cross does not publish its findings but instead shares them with the government and tries to convince it to change its ways.

The Bush administration ignored a series of critical Red Cross reports issued from October 2003 into 2004, which included personal appeals to National Security Adviser Rice and CPA chief Bremer to stop the torture, humiliation, and other abuses. Evidence of torture was leaking despite the White House's attempts to cover up the systematic abuses of human rights. Some of the soldiers involved in the humiliations proudly posted photos of their deeds on the Internet. Then, on January 13, 2004, an enlisted man, who both understood and had the courage to act upon his legal duties as an American soldier and citizen, formally submitted evidence of these crimes to military officials. This forced General Sanchez to order a formal but secret inquiry.

Before the Internet era, an "inquiry" might have simply hushed up the matter. But countless pieces of evidence were floating through cyberspace, and it was only a matter of time before they became lead stories in newspapers and television broadcasts. CBS's *60 Minutes* first broke the story on April 28, 2004. The show provoked a mass media investigation that uncovered hundreds of disturbing photos and written accounts of widespread tormenting and outright torture. Billions of people around the world were shocked and horrified by those crimes. And the photos served as recruitment posters for terrorists set on inflicting vengeance.

Yet, more than the Bush team's heavy-handed tactics pushed Iraqis into the ranks of the insurgents. The Iraqi government could be just as inept. Its handling of the trial and execution of Saddam Hussein managed to turn him into a martyr rather than a villain for many Iraqis, including even some Shiites who had otherwise hated him.

Saddam and eleven other high-ranking officials had been handed over from American to Iraqi control on June 30, 2004, two days after the transfer of power from the CPA to the Iraqi government.

Via television and the Internet, the world watched as he stayed defiant to the end. He argued with judges and lawyers during the months of a show trial until the judges declared him guilty of murder and ordered his execution. On December 30, 2006, as he stood on the gallows with a noose around his neck, he denounced his enemies and praised Allah before a crowd of jeering, black-hooded men. Then someone pulled the trapdoor's lever, and in an instant the tyrant dangled in space with his neck broken.

The trial and execution aided Islamists and Ba'athists alike in two ways. Critics condemned the show trial for violating international legal standards and ending before Saddam was confronted with the entire array of charges against him. His execution then revealed a courageous Saddam, defiant before a lynch mob. In the hearts and minds of hundreds of millions around the world, Saddam appeared as a victim rather than the evil mass murderer of before.

All of this could have been avoided had the Bush administration handed Saddam over to the International Criminal Court at the Hague for a proper trial. But that would have been a gross violation of ideological correctness, since conservatives despise international laws and organizations. Thus, what could have been a great propaganda coup for the United States and the international community instead played into the hands of America's worst enemies.

As the death and destruction worsened, the Bush administration stayed the "search, destroy, withdraw" strategic course. Surveys revealed that the United States was clearly losing the battle for hearts and minds. By virtually every measure the misery, anti-American, and pro-Islamism indexes soared. A September 2006 poll found that 71 percent of Iraqis wanted the United States to leave within a year, with 65 percent of them preferring an immediate withdrawal. According to a March 2007 poll, 51 percent of all Iraqis and 90 percent of all Sunnis approved of attacks on Coalition forces![8]

TABLE 17.1   Survey of Iraqi Attitudes

LIFE TODAY COMPARED TO BEFORE THE WAR	2007	2005	2004
Much better	14%	21%	22%
Somewhat better	29%	31%	35%
About the same	22%	19%	23%
Somewhat worse	28%	19%	13%
Much worse	8%	10%	6%
No response/Don't know	1%	2%	

THE AMERICAN-LED INVASION	2007	2005	2004
Absolutely right	22%	19%	20%
Somewhat right	25%	28%	29%
Somewhat wrong	19%	17%	13%
Absolutely wrong	34%	33%	26%
Refused/Don't know	—	4%	13%

RECONSTRUCTION EFFORTS	2007	2005
Very effective	6%	18%
Quite effective	27%	18%
Quite ineffective	35%	14%
Very ineffective	23%	26%
No efforts	9%	12%
Don't know/Not needed	1%	12%

EVALUATE COALITION	2007	2005
Very good job	6%	10%
Quite a good job	18%	27%
Quite a bad job	30%	19%
A very bad job	46%	40%

(continued)

TABLE 17.1 *(continued)*

FEELINGS TOWARD COALITION	2007	2005	2004	
Strongly support	6%	13%	13%	
Somewhat support	16%	19%	26%	
Somewhat oppose	32%	21%	20%	
Strongly oppose	46%	44%	31%	
Refused/Don't know	—	3%	10%	

US AND UK OCCUPATION FORCES	2007	2005	2004	2003
Great deal of confidence	6%	7%	8%	7%
Quite a lot of confidence	12%	11%	17%	12%
Not very much confidence	30%	23%	23%	20%
None at all	52%	55%	43%	52%
Refused/Don't know	—	5%	8%	9%

EFFECT OF U.S. FORCES ON IRAQI SECURITY (2007)	BETTER	WORSE	NO EFFECT
	21%	69%	10%

U.S. ROLE IN IRAQ (2007)	POSITIVE	NEUTRAL	NEGATIVE
	12%	11%	77%

	ACCEPTABLE	UNACCEPTABLE	REFUSE/DON'T KNOW
ATTACKS ON COALITION FORCES (2007)	51%	49%	—
ATTACKS ON GOVERNMENT FORCES (2007)	12%	88%	—

SEPARATION OF PEOPLE BY SECTARIANISM (2007)	GOOD	BAD	REFUSED/DON'T KNOW
	6%	94%	—

BEST FOR IRAQ NOW	2007	2005	2004
Strong leader: one man for life	34%	26%	28%
Islamic state	22%	14%	21%
Democracy	43%	57%	49%
Refused/Don't know	—	3%	4%

BEST FOR IRAQ FIVE YEARS LATER	2007	2005
Strong leader: one man for life	26%	18%
Islamic state	22%	12%
Democracy	53%	64%
Refused/Don't know	—	7%

Poll conducted by D3 Systems for the BBC, ABC News, ARD German TV, and USA Today of more than 2,000 people in 450 neighborhoods and villages across all eighteen Iraqi provinces between February 25 and March 5, 2007. The earlier polls used similar methodologies.

The Bush team reacted to the sinking poll figures in Iraq with the same strategy they used in the United States. They tried to manipulate Iraqi public opinion by planting stories in the print and electronic media, often paying journalists and editors handsomely for the privilege. That tactic worked only until the practice was revealed. The result was to discredit Iraq's mass media as nothing more than a loudspeaker for the Bush administration.

The Pew Global Attitudes Project revealed differences within the Muslim world in reaction to Bush administration policies and other global events and trends. Of six mostly Muslim countries, America's standing fell in Egypt from 30 percent to 22 percent, in Turkey from 52 percent to 12 percent, in Jordan from 25 percent to 19 percent, and in Indonesia from 75 percent to 37 percent, but actually rose in Lebanon from 36 percent to 51 percent and in Nigeria from 46 percent to 64 percent, although the span of Bush years varied.

The World Public Opinion Survey published in 2007, found deeply entrenched anti-Americanism in four key Muslim countries whose governments generally work closely with the United States:

TABLE 17.2   Views of the Current (2007) U.S. Government

	FAVORABLE	UNFAVORABLE
Morocco	16%	76%
Egypt	4%	93%
Pakistan	15%	67%
Indonesia	20%	66%

U.S. GOAL IS TO WEAKEN AND DIVIDE ISLAM

	DEFINITELY/PROBABLY	DEFINITELY NOT/PROBABLY NOT
Morocco	78%	11%
Egypt	92%	4%
Pakistan	73%	9%
Indonesia	73%	15%

U.S. GOAL IS TO SPREAD CHRISTIANITY

	DEFINITELY/PROBABLY	DEFINITELY NOT/PROBABLY NOT
Morocco	67%	22%
Pakistan	64%	14%
Indonesia	61%	21%

(continued)

TABLE 17.2 *(continued)*

PRIMARY GOAL OF U.S. WAR ON TERROR

	TO WEAKEN, DIVIDE MUSLIMS	POLITICAL, MILITARY DOMINATION OF MIDDLE EAST OIL	TO PROTECT ITSELF FROM TERRORISM
Morocco	33%	39%	19%
Egypt	31%	55%	9%
Pakistan	42%	26%	12%
Indonesia	29%	24%	23%

APPROVAL OF ATTACKS ON U.S. TROOPS IN IRAQ

	APPROVE	MIXED FEELINGS	DISAPPROVE
Morocco	68%	11%	14%
Egypt	91%	2%	4%
Pakistan	35%	13%	35%
Indonesia	19%	11%	61%

APPROVAL OF ATTACKS ON U.S. TROOPS IN AFGHANISTAN

	APPROVE	MIXED FEELINGS	DISAPPROVE
Morocco	61%	14%	17%
Egypt	91%	2%	4%
Pakistan	34%	14%	33%
Indonesia	19%	10%	59%

APPROVAL OF ATTACKS ON U.S. TROOPS IN PERSIAN GULF

	APPROVE	MIXED FEELINGS	DISAPPROVE
Morocco	52%	19%	17%
Egypt	83%	3%	10%
Pakistan	32%	14%	57%

Nonetheless Al Qaeda and its affiliates do have some vulnerabilities, as revealed by surveys of selected Muslim countries. The World Public Opinion Survey of 2007 found mixed attitudes toward Al Qaeda in particular and terrorism in general:

TABLE 17.3 Groups Such as Al Qaeda Using Violence against Civilians

	AGREE	DISAGREE
Morocco	66%	19%
Egypt	88%	7%
Pakistan	30%	35%
Indonesia	65%	21%

(continued)

TABLE 17.3 *(continued)*

SUPPORT FOR SUICIDE ATTACKS AGAINST AN ENEMY

	OFTEN JUSTIFIED	SOMETIMES JUSTIFIED	RARELY JUSTIFIED	NEVER JUSTIFIED
Morocco	16%	19%	19%	34%
Egypt	41%	19%	8%	28%
Pakistan	6%	11	11%	62%
Indonesia	3%	12	13%	68%

ATTACKS ON CIVILIANS IN AMERICA

	APPROVE	MIXED FEELINGS	DISAPPROVE
Morocco	7%	8%	78%
Egypt	6%	2%	91%
Pakistan	5%	13%	67%
Indonesia	4%	7%	75%

ATTACKS ON CIVILIANS IN EUROPE

	APPROVE	MIXED FEELINGS	DISAPPROVE
Morocco	6%	7%	82%
Egypt	4%	2%	93%
Pakistan	6%	14%	63%
Indonesia	3%	5%	78%

ATTACKS ON U.S. CIVILIANS WORKING FOR U.S. COMPANIES IN MUSLIM COUNTRIES

	APPROVE	MIXED FEELINGS	DISAPPROVE
Morocco	7%	13%	73%
Egypt	6%	2%	90%
Pakistan	7%	16%	58%
Indonesia	3%	7%	76%

FEELINGS TOWARD OSAMA BIN LADEN

	POSITIVE	MIXED	NEGATIVE
Morocco	27%	26%	21%
Egypt	40%	34%	20%
Pakistan	27%	24%	15%
Indonesia	21%	32%	19%

EFFECTS OF 9/11 ON ISLAMIC WORLD

	POSITIVE	MIXED	NEGATIVE
Morocco	12%	13%	62%
Egypt	23%	3%	70%
Pakistan	8%	6%	50%
Indonesia	19%	4%	56%

(continued)

TABLE 17.3 *(continued)*

SUPPORT FOR GROUPS THAT ATTACK AMERICANS

	DISAPPROVE	APPROVE OF SOME	APPROVE OF ALL
Morocco	44%	35%	3%
Egypt	26%	51%	15%
Pakistan	43%	10%	5%
Indonesia	52%	18%	6%

VIEWS OF AL QAEDA	AVERAGE	MOROCCO	EGYPT	PAKISTAN	INDONESIA
Support attacks on U.S. and share its attitudes toward U.S.	23%	31%	31%	7%	24%
Oppose its attacks but share many attitudes toward U.S.	26%	26%	31%	17%	29%
Oppose its attacks and do not share its attitudes	37%	35%	14%	66%	32%

As for general values, the respondents overwhelmingly cherished traditional Islamic values and rejected Western values:

TABLE 17.4　Goal to Keep Western Values out of Muslim Countries

	AGREE STRONGLY	AGREE SOMEWHAT	DISAGREE
Morocco	33%	1%	64%
Egypt	80%	11%	91%
Pakistan	45%	22%	67%
Indonesia	40%	38%	78%

GOAL TO STRICTLY APPLY FOR SHARIA IN ALL MUSLIM COUNTRIES

	AGREE STRONGLY	AGREE SOMEWHAT	DISAGREE
Morocco	35%	41%	76%
Egypt	50%	24%	74%
Pakistan	54%	25%	79%
Indonesia	17%	36%	53%

The disastrous results of the conservative crusade for American security as revealed by surveys were not confined to the Middle East, but were nearly global. This might have been true even if the Bush team had been a paragon rather than pariah of international law, morality, moderation, and wisdom. But more than two years of the Bush team's contempt and defiance of international law and gratuitous insults to allies and adversaries alike had provoked an ever fiercer anti-Americanism around the world.

The Pew Global Attitudes Project revealed that the number of countries with favorable views of the United States plummeted during the Bush years, although there were some exceptions. The approval of America's three key European allies all dropped sharply from 2000 to 2008, with Britain falling from 83 percent to 53 percent, Germany from 78 percent to 31 percent, and France from 62 percent to 42 percent. As a result, many formal allies either limited their support or shuffled along reluctantly and red-faced with White House demands.

Central to those attitudes was the feeling that the United States was blatantly violating international laws of war. Were those perceptions correct?

That body of laws addresses three crucial questions: Is the war just? Is the war fought justly? Is the war resolved justly?[9]

A score of treaties have elaborated the legal and illegal ways to fight a war. International laws of war accept the reality that innocent people will die. Those deaths would violate international law only if the innocents were either deliberately targeted or no efforts were made to minimize their deaths.

The Pentagon was careful to fight its wars in both Afghanistan and Iraq as justly as possible by adhering to international law, especially by doing all it could to minimize civilian casualties, the so-called collateral damage. But then the Bush team undercut that effort with its policy of violating the international laws prohibiting incarceration without charges or trial, humiliation, and torture of prisoners. People around the world were sickened by the hundreds of photos of American soldiers tormenting Iraqi prisoners at Abu Ghraib. Countless people associated those evils not just with the Bush team, but with America. And America's enemies everywhere rejoiced.

War is justified under international law under very narrow circumstances: preempting an imminent attack, defending against an attack, and being authorized to go to war by the UN Security Council. By that standard, the Bush administration's wars in Afghanistan and Iraq could not have legally differed more. Mainstream experts conclude that the United States fought a just war in Afghanistan and an unjust war in Iraq.[10]

The case for going to war in Afghanistan was legally supported. Al Qaeda declared war on the United States in 1996 and 1998, and launched murderous attacks on Americans in 1998, 2000, and 2001. Although Al Qaeda fielded thousands of operatives in about eighty countries, its headquarters was in Afghanistan. The Taliban, the Islamist revolutionary movement that ruled Afghanistan, refused White House demands that it surrender Osama bin Laden and all others responsible for the September 11 attacks.

As for the war against Iraq, the conservatives justified their war on grounds of "preemption" against an imminent attack. That assertion was easily exposed as nonsense. The Gulf War of 1991, followed by the UN's anti-WMD policies, and a dozen years of economic sanctions had destroyed the Iraqi military's capacity to be a serious threat against its neighbors let alone the United States over seven thousand miles away.

When challenged with the reality, most war supporters then explained that while Iraq might not pose an immediate threat to the United States, it could pose a future threat if it somehow evaded all the sanctions and built WMDs. They called such a policy a "preventive war." But here again ideology ran smack into insurmountable barriers of logic and law. The future could not be predicted. They were advocating a war to prevent something that quite likely would never have happened. Under international law and by the norms of morality, such a war would have been an illegal act of imperialism, defined as the conquest and transformation of one state by another.

Finally, the Bush team claimed that their war was justified under UN Security Council resolutions 1441 and 678, along with fourteen others that were evoked against Iraq from 1990 to 2002. This logic was curious to say the least. In fact, none of those resolutions either individually or collectively specifically empowered the United States to go to war against the Iraq. For instance, Resolution 678, which passed on November 29, 1990, called on all UN members to "use all necessary means" to get Iraq to withdraw from Kuwait and "restore international peace and security in the area." The Gulf War fulfilled Resolution 678 by not only expelling Iraq's army from Kuwait, but destroying Iraq's offensive military capacity. The subsequent UN inspections eliminated Iraq's WMD programs. Resolution 678 was legally a dead letter.

No one government has the right to unilaterally interpret and act upon a UN resolution unless it is empowered by the UN Security Council to do so. It is the Security Council's duty to declare exactly what means are necessary under what circumstances. Until it does so, that resolution is suspended. Secretary-General Kofi Annan stated that America's war against Iraq was "not in conformity with the Security Council, with the U.N. Charter . . . . From the Charter's point of view, it was illegal." As if that was not powerful enough, Pope John Paul II grounded this legal argument in morality by repeatedly denouncing the Iraq War as "a crime against peace."[11]

None of that seemed to faze the conservatives who were either indifferent or outright hostile to such "liberal" nonsense as "winning hearts and minds" or "nation-building." That attitude is vividly expressed by the conservative slogan that "if you grab 'em by the balls their hearts and minds will follow!"

Yet conservatives had increasing trouble ignoring or dismissing an even more wrenching shift in hearts and minds at home. The ever worsening cost in blood and treasure, capped by revelations of massive corruption and the Abu Ghraib scandal, turned increasing numbers of Americans from fervent supporters to skeptics or outright critics. Nonetheless, there remained a hard core of true believers who never lost faith in the conservative crusade in Iraq.

Not surprisingly, all along evangelical Christians were the most credulous when it came to blindly following the Bush administration's policies, values, and beliefs. In a 2004 analysis in *Political Science Quarterly* titled "Misperceptions, the Media, and the Iraq War," the authors compared beliefs according to two criteria.[12] One was which television network the respondents watched for news. The other was whether they were evangelical Republicans, non-evangelical Republicans, and non-evangelical Democrats. Three questions were asked: (1) whether world opinion favored the war; (2) whether evidence of an Al Qaeda link was found; and, (3) whether WMDs were found.

The results for which television station one watched were hardly surprising but nonetheless revealing. The greatest percentage of misinformed Americans were devotees of the right-wing Fox News Network, with an average ignorance rate of 45 percent for getting all three questions wrong. The lowest average was for PBS viewers, with only a 12 percent ignorance rate. The ignorance rate for the other broadcasters that were once centrist but had leaned to the right—ABC, CNN, NBC, and CBS—varied from 30 percent (ABC) to 35 percent (CBS).

TABLE 17.5

	REPUBLICAN EVANGELICALS	REPUBLICAN NON-EVANGELICALS	DEMOCRAT NON-EVANGELICALS
Believe Saddam had WMDs	81.5%	63.4%	36.5%
Believe Saddam link with 9/11	57.9%	49.3%	32.6%
Believe Bush did not exaggerate claims	75.8%	66.4%	20.2%
Believe Bush did not mislead nation to war against Iraq	89.7%	78.8%	26.7%
Believe U.S. was right to war against Iraq	88.3%	78.8%	63.2%
Believe Iraq War is worth cost	72.4%	63.2% ·	16.1%

TABLE 17.6

	REPUBLICAN EVANGELICALS	REPUBLICAN NON-EVANGELICALS	DEMOCRAT NON-EVANGELICALS
Iraq War was just	89.7%	81.2%	22.7%
Iraq War was worth cost	88.5%	71.3%	25.2%
Acceptable number of U.S. casualties	63.7%	47.8%	13.5%
Iraq War enhances U.S. security	84.4%	73.1%	35.1%
U.S. making progress in Iraq	70.8%	60.7%	17.9%
Keep troops in Iraq till job is done	86.6%	78.4%	40.0%
Things are going very well or well	86.2%	74.8%	24.5%\
Very or somewhat confident Iraq will be stable in a year	67.8%	60.3%	24.7%
Insurgency on last legs	48.3%	37.8%	29.1%

The differences among the evangelical Republicans, non-evangelical Republicans, and non-evangelical Democrats were just as predicable.

Over time, the ratio between blind believers and critical thinkers shifted. Not surprisingly nearly two-thirds of Americans believed there was a trade-off between liberty and security in the months following 9/11. However, by July 2003, 55 percent opposed that notion while only 44 percent supported it. That reversal is most likely explained by revelations of the Bush team's ham-fisted tactics that raised troubling constitutional, legal, and moral questions.[13]

American support for the Iraq War fell faster than it did for the Vietnam War, even though casualties for the former were only a fraction of those for the latter, while the Bush administration did everything in its power to prevent the public from seeing images of body bags, flag-draped coffins, funerals, and mutilated survivors. What explains that tidal shift in public opinion? Some argue that the American public is not "casualty-phobic" but "defeat-phobic" and thus are willing to endure the human costs of war as long as they are winning. Although the Vietnam syndrome—or an aversion to fighting prolonged wars against anti-American movements when no discernable rational vital American interests are threatened—was dead following the easy victory of the 1991 Gulf War and the horrors of 9/11, it was not buried and increasingly began to reemerge. Comparisons of Iraq with the unwinnable war in Vietnam grew more virulent as the insurgency worsened and the corruption, incompetence, and brutality of the American occupation grew apparent.[14]

Three of four Americans supported the Iraq War in 2003. While there was a steady decline from that height, the tipping point came in late 2005 as the conservative crusade bogged down into an ever bloodier quagmire. Support for the Bush team's policies thereafter steadily declined. Democrats retook both houses of Congress in the 2006 elections and strengthened their hold over Congress and won the White House in the 2008 elections. A December 2008 poll by ABC News and the *Washington Post* found that 64 percent now believed that the Iraq War had been a mistake, while 34 percent believed that it was worth fighting, and 2 percent were undecided.[15]

In the end, the conservatives lost their war for American hearts and minds, but not before they had manipulated the mainstream media and public opinion into supporting disastrous policies that severely damaged American security, power, wealth, and honor.

18

The Surge

The war's turning point came when the Bush administration changed its strategy from "search, destroy, and withdraw" to "clear, hold, and build," and from "killing or capturing insurgents" to "securing and nurturing the population."

That shift in strategy originated with a coalition of realists on the ground in Iraq and in Washington, backed by plummeting public support for the war. These forces coalesced in early 2006 and eventually dragged the Bush team to adopt what became known as the "surge" strategy in early 2007.

Public opinion was essential to that policy shift. While the conservatives insisted that victory was just around the corner in Iraq, increasing numbers of Americans grew skeptical as the war's body count and bill soared. The president's approval ratings sank steadily as his administration bungled not just the Iraq crusade, but an array of other issues. By January 2006, nearly two-thirds of Americans disapproved, and only one-third approved, of Bush's performance as president, and a solid majority now believed that the United States should never have invaded Iraq, was creating more Islamist enemies the longer it stayed, and should find a way to extract itself as soon as possible.

These poll numbers emboldened congressional realists. On March 15, 2006, over the White House's bitter protests, Congress appointed a ten-person, bipartisan group of realists led by James Baker and Lee Hamilton, former congressman and vice chairman of the 9/11 Commission, to evaluate the current Iraq policy, its consequences, and reasonable alternatives. This Iraq Study Group issued its report on December 6, 2006. In contrast to all the conservative happy talk, the realists explained that "the situation in Iraq is grave and deteriorating." They then offered seventy-nine recommendations for a new strategy. There was no talk of victory or a democratic revolution. Instead, the White House should seek a diplomatic deal both among the major factions within Iraq and among the surrounding countries, including Iran and Syria, that would end the fighting and promote stability as the United States steadily drew down its forces.[1]

The Bush administration rejected these policies as defeatist. But in the White House a bitter consensus was emerging that something new was necessary. As early as November 2005, an analysis began circulating within the administration with two key strategic concepts in which to ground the new policy: "clear, hold, and build" and "as Iraqi forces stand up, we will stand down."

These ideas reflected innovative strategies in Iraq and in military journal articles by such as generals Peter Chiarelli, Mark Hertling, Stanley McChrystal, and David Petraeus. For instance, General Hertling, who commanded coalition forces across northern Iraq, found a way to counter the escalating female suicide bombings. He organized a woman's conference in Arbil, where many of the bombers originated, challenged the participants to change the political culture, and asked for volunteers to join the police force. Armed with a list of potential recruits, he then went to the police chief and pressured him into accepting women into the police force. This gave women an alternative model, while allowing the police a female force with which to search female terrorist suspects.[2]

No one contributed more to the new strategy than Gen. David Petraeus, a brilliant theorist and practitioner of counterinsurgency warfare.[3] He graduated in the top 5 percent of his West Point class and number one in his class at Ft. Leavenworth's command school, and got a doctorate in international relations from Princeton University. Yet he was a soldier's soldier who excelled during Ranger and paratrooper training and liked challenging his troops to pushup contests. As the commander of the 101st Airborne Division, he had successfully quelled a rebellion around Mosul in northern Iraq. He was asked to assemble and oversee a team of experts to write the joint army and Marine Corps counterinsurgency manual, which would appear in 2006.

Petraeus was appointed Iraq's ground commander on January 5, 2007, and was given 31,000 reinforcements, which, once those five brigades were deployed a half year later, would bring the number of American troops to around 160,000. That "surge" involved an array of interrelated essential elements. Since even those fresh troops were far short of what was needed to secure the entire country, Petraeus concentrated them in Baghdad, Iraq's largest city. Combined forces of American and Iraqi troops would secure Baghdad's population neighborhood by neighborhood with enough troops to kill or drive out the insurgents. Special efforts were made to find and capture insurgent leaders. Then, rather than withdraw to the safety of a base, the troops would stay while aid organizations began restoring such basic needs as running water, sewage, electricity, roads, schools, and so on.

That strategy gradually transformed the population's bunker mentality back to a market mentality. People had the safety and thus the confidence with which to reopen their businesses, go shopping, and send their children to school. Meanwhile, the Americans would train, equip, and deploy more Iraqi soldiers and police to take over security. And gradually people began to see the American forces as protectors rather than as brutal repressors and destroyers. The insurgency withered, with ever fewer recruits and refugees. In all, the surge was a stunning success. Violence, death, and destruction dropped significantly. For instance, around nine thousand roadside bombs either exploded or were defused in 2008, an alarming number until it is compared to the thirty thousand in 2006.[4]

Several factors contributed to that success beyond the surge's blueprint. The vicious ethnic cleansing that had caused countless numbers of deaths and refugees left the survivors relatively secure in the turf that they were able to seize and hold by killing or driving off their rivals. This would have resulted in a significant fall-off in violence even without the surge.

Then, among Sunnis, Al Qaeda managed to exceed the Bush administration in the sheer ineptness of its policies. Al Qaeda alienated Sunnis by indiscriminately murdering them while killing Shiites to provoke war between the sects. It also imposed harsh Taliban-style restrictions on Sunni women and publicly beat those who did not comply. In some places it kidnapped people for ransom. By the time Abu Musaab al-Zarqawi was run to ground and killed on June 7, 2006, most of the Sunni groups that had originally embraced Al Qaeda had turned their guns against it. Abu Ayoub al-Masri, an Egyptian who took over Al Qaeda after al-Zarqawi's death, has been much more low-profile than his predecessor. Nonetheless, on October 15, 2006, several Sunni groups once affiliated with Al Qaeda announced their separation from that group and the formation of "the Islamic State of Iraq."

Another American advantage was the lack of unified command among the insurgents. More often than not a multistranded war raged, with an array of groups trying to kill each other as well as the Americans. General Petraeus took full advantage of these divisions with a policy of playing off the militias against one another and renting their loyalty.

Those groups that allied with the Americans became known as Awakening Councils that collectively became known as the Awakening Movement. The movement began in Anbar Province, which once was among the insurgency's hotbeds. Anbar is predominately Sunni, so the tribes and clans there could concentrate on killing Americans. The first Awakening Council emerged in November 2005 when the Abu Mahal tribe allied with the United States. It did so both from the push of Al Qaeda's atrocities and the pull of American inducements of money, guns, training, and protection. In September 2006 the tribe began calling itself the "Anbar Awakening Council." Eventually thirty-five tribes and clans joined. That security gave men confidence to work for the government; within a few months the ranks of the police alone rose from 200 to 7,400.[5]

While the Awakening Movement led to sharp falls in violence where the councils have emerged, there were potential problems. The most troubling for the Shiite-dominated Iraqi government was that the Sunni militias were a rival military force to the Iraqi army. Baghdad hoped to integrate about a third of the groups into the regular army as "Sons of Iraq." Another possible pitfall was that the Awakening councils were allied with the United States solely to help defend themselves from Al Qaeda, Shiite militias, and often each other. The result was essentially a mercenary relationship whereby the United States trained, armed, and financed tribal militias in return for tenuous alliances. The shorthand term for this policy was "cash for cooperation." These groups would not have hesitated to turn their guns on American forces if it was in their interest to do so. But for the time being, they held their fire.

19

Empowering Iran

One final essential factor explains the surge's success: Iran. Indeed, if the conservative crusade in Iraq has a clear winner, it is Iran. The Bush team could not have played Tehran's game better if they had let Iran's supreme leader, the Ayatollah Ali Khamenei, dictate the policy.

Sandwiched between Afghanistan and Iraq, Iran is acutely sensitive to regional events and has been a key player in both its neighbors' conflicts. With Afghanistan's Taliban and Al Qaeda, the United States and Iran shared common enemies, while the conservatives and mullahs both sought to destroy Saddam Hussein's regime. The Iranians saw the American wars in Afghanistan and Iraq as godsends by eliminating Iran's enemies. Iranian revolutionaries are filling the subsequent political vacuums in both countries.[1] Iran's power over Iraq was perhaps best symbolized by what happened after Iraq's second democratic election, held March 7, 2010. The three parties that won the largest number of parliamentary seats sent delegations to Iran to receive its revolutionary government's blessing and advice. But none of those delegations went to Washington, which had destroyed Saddam's dictatorship and built a democratic system on its ruins. Two of these parties— Prime Minister Nuri Kamal Maliki's State of Law Coalition and radical cleric Moktada al-Sadr's Iraqi National Alliance—were openly Islamist, anti-Western, and beholden to Iran. But even the Western-leaning Iraqiya Party led by Ayad Allawi had to pay homage to the real power behind the American façade in Iraq.[2]

The Iraq War destroyed, in favor of Tehran, the region's power balance between Iran and Iraq, respectively a revolutionary Islamist Persian regime and a secular Arab dictatorship. As a result, Tehran enjoys greater influence over Iraq. Six of ten Iraqis are Shiites, and their primary loyalty is to their version of Islam rather than to their Arab ethnicity. Iran's elite Quds Force has not only organized, financed, trained, and armed all the major Shiite groups and tens of thousands of militants, but has also infiltrated countless sleeper cells in Iraq. Tehran has the power to worsen or diminish the Shiite insurgency in Iraq. And recently, the Iranian government has been reaching out to some Sunni militants as well. Guided by the classic strategy "the enemy of my enemy is my friend," Tehran has tolerated the transit or refuge of Al Qaeda operatives, money, and arms. Reports surfaced in spring 2008 that Tehran and Al Qaeda were conducting secret talks.[3]

Tehran could not massively infiltrate Iraq while Saddam Hussein was in power. It could, however, insidiously plant and nurture revolutionary movements in softer targets. As early as 1981, Tehran set up an Islamic Revolutionary Council to recruit, fund, train, arm, shelter, and dispatch Islamist militants to foster revolution across the Muslim world and beyond. One State Department study of the groups that Tehran sponsored found that nearly nine of ten were Shiite, one of ten were Sunni, and only one of a hundred were in the "other" category. The most successful Islamist group that Tehran's Revolutionary Guards helped found and nurture was Hezbollah, or the Party of God, in Lebanon in the early 1980s. A series of Hezbollah attacks against the United States in Lebanon in 1983 and 1984 forced the Reagan administration into a humiliating retreat and concessions. Since the United States destroyed Saddam Hussein's regime, Hezbollah has embedded itself ever deeper across Iraq's Shiite communities.[4]

Iran poses not just a revolutionary Islamist threat to the region. Nuclear weapons will soon back those militant Islamists steadily spreading across the Middle East. Iran is developing a nuclear energy industry with the capacity to convert enriched uranium or plutonium into nuclear weapons. That nuclear complex is buried deep underground in numerous sites ringed by troops and surface-to-air missiles. By early 2009 Iran had enough enriched uranium to build a nuclear bomb. It was also busy developing the missiles that could deliver such a nuclear bomb. With a 1,300-kilometer range, Iran's Shahab-3 missile can target Israel.[5]

Iran's militants and nuclear weapons protect each other. Should the United States or Israel attack Iran's nuclear complex, Tehran would call on its Quds Force, Hezbollah, and other Shiite militants to wage jihad against American forces in Iraq and Afghanistan, while similar uprisings would erupt in a half-dozen other countries across the region. Iranian militants are mushrooming under the shadow of Iran's growing nuclear power.

Tehran's power against the United States extends far beyond its ability to provoke anti-American insurgencies in Iraq within the Shiite population and in Afghanistan among Farsi speakers. Iran is often said to have America and its allies over a barrel—an oil barrel, that is. Clearly the country with the world's third largest oil reserves has enormous potential power to turn off and on the spigot to a world economy that runs on oil.

Tehran's physical power is not confined to pumping petroleum from the earth. With 65 million people, 540,000 troops, arms distributed among 5.9 million people, and a territory slightly larger than Alaska, Iran would be far more difficult to defeat and occupy than Iraq, whose military power had been degraded by decades of war and sanctions.

Iran, however, is far from omnipotent. Chronic and worsening economic problems undercut Iran's military power. The population is growing much faster than the economy and is plagued by ever worsening unemployment, inflation, and poverty. Tehran's failure to diversify its economy away from dependence on oil means that revenues soar or plunge with oil prices. As the economy erodes, Tehran must spend more of its revenues on welfare rather than on the investments that might diversify and upgrade the economy. The UN economic sanctions are further eroding Iran's economy as desperately needed goods and capital are withheld. These shortages are especially acute in Iran's oil industry, whose productivity is falling steadily to the point where exports may end in 2015. Indeed, Iran must import gasoline because it lacks oil refineries. This would be Iranian Achilles' heel should a war break out.[6]

The mass protests following the rigged presidential election of June 12, 2009, which kept Mahmoud Ahmadinejad in power, revealed the depth and breadth of anger against Tehran. The clerics split, with most supporting the election results, some condemning them, and still others watching warily from the sidelines. Most of those who joined the protests were not Western-style liberals, but were instead anti-Western Islamists who wanted economic and political reforms. Eventually, the government was able to suppress the protests.

Given Iran's power in the Middle East, President Barack Obama recognized that the United States had no realistic choice but to talk. In his inaugural address, he eloquently offered to "extend a hand" to Tehran, along with other enemies, if it would "unclench its fist." In another speech, he lauded Iranian culture and welcomed "the Islamic Republic of Iran to take its rightful place in the community of nations."[7] So far President Ahmadinejad has not taken those offers.

20
Winners and Losers

While Iran and a handful of American corporations made out like bandits, the conservative crusade in Iraq devastated American national security, power, wealth, and honor. The Bush team saddled Americans with a Texas-sized country teeming with 24 million mostly impoverished, traumatized, and angry inhabitants. By November 2008 the Iraq War was costing the United States $10 billion a month, with a worsening array of liabilities and no discernable beneficiaries other than carpetbagging corporations.

While conservatives argue that the surge's success and the 2010 Iraqi election has vindicated their policies, from a realist perspective the United States lost the Iraq War the day the invasion began on March 19, 2003. That invasion destroyed what had been a successful, relatively low-cost triple containment policy. The America-led coalition and the UN Security Council had contained Iraq through the 1991 Gulf War sanctions and WMD inspection and dismantlement programs. In turn, Iraq brutally contained Islamism within its borders as well as Iran beyond its eastern frontier. The result was a stable power balance in the Persian Gulf. The Bush administration destroyed all that by destroying Saddam Hussein and his brutal regime, and thus grossly damaged American national security.

The Bush team's initial policies in Iraq presented a perfect model for how to feed an insurgency. The American occupation's corruption, ineptness, and brutality alienated millions of Iraqis, turned thousands into insurgents and terrorists, and squandered hundreds of billions of dollars, tens of thousands of Iraqi lives, and thousands of American lives. The Bush team had wielded enough military power to destroy Saddam's regime but deployed only a fraction of that necessary to control the country. By comparison, if the same ratio of occupation forces were deployed in Iraq as NATO had in Bosnia, the White House would have somehow had to scrap up half a million troops for Iraq![1]

Like virtually all terrorism experts, Jessica Stern laments that in Iraq "America has created . . . precisely the situation that the Bush administration has described as a breeding ground for terrorists: a state unable to control its borders or provide for its citizens' rudimentary needs. . . . As bad as the situation inside Iraq may be, the effect that the war has had on terrorist recruitment around the world may be even more worrisome. . . . America has taken a country that was not a terrorist threat and turned it into one." Peter Bergen and Paul Cruikshank estimate that the Iraq War "has generated a stunning seven-fold increase in the yearly rate of fatal jihadist attacks, amounting to literally hundreds of additional terrorist attacks and thousands of civilian victims." The 2006 National Intelligence Estimate reached the same dark conclusion: "The Iraq conflict has become the cause célèbre for jihadists, breeding a deep resentment of US involvement in the Muslim world and cultivating supporters for the global jihadist movement."[2]

The human costs were also staggering. By the time the Bush team left office, the coalition forces alone had suffered the deaths of 4,222 American service members and 315 other foreign troops, of whom 178 were British. Wounded Americans numbered 30,920, of whom 20 percent suffered serious brain or spinal injuries. As for deep emotional wounds, three of ten soldiers developed serious mental health problems or "post-traumatic stress disorder" (PTSD) within several months of returning home. Not only men and women in uniform were killed while serving in Iraq. By July 2008, 1,186 civilian contractors, of whom 244 were Americans, had also died.[3]

Appalling as those numbers are, they are overshadowed by the Iraqi dead and maimed. At first it was difficult to get statistics on the number of Iraqi soldiers, insurgents, or civilians killed in the fighting. Gen. Tommy Franks summed up the White House policy as "We don't do body counts." Soldiers in the field put it more colorfully as a policy of "shoot, shovel, and shove on." Franks later dropped his reticence and reckoned that about thirty thousand Iraqi soldiers and civilians had died by April 9, 2003.[4]

The Pentagon would eventually proudly report that American and allied troops were eliminating more of the enemy. The total number of known insurgents killed in Iraq from 2003 through July 2007 was 10,190, with 315 killed in 2003, 3,732 in 2004, 1,365 in 2004, 1,701 in 2006, and 3,077 in the first half of 2007. By a different calculation, 18,832 insurgents were killed in combat from 2003 through August 2007, while over 25,000 insurgents were prisoners. The downside of those statistics, of course, was that the number of insurgents was growing faster than the number getting killed, a fact that the Pentagon was not as eager to cite.[5]

The number of Iraqi soldiers and policemen killed in the fighting rose steadily as the occupation trained and deployed more of them. Iraqi security forces suffered 8,745 deaths from June 2003 through November 5, 2008. If recruits killed while in training are included, the figure rises to 11,057.[6]

The Iraqi people, of course, bore the war's worst devastation. As for civilian deaths, the Pentagon remained tight-lipped, especially as the insurgency worsened and the number of dead and maimed in all categories soared. Eventually, other organizations and ministries began trying to come up with figures of just how many Iraqis had died directly or indirectly because of the war. The accuracy, however, was questionable as each used its own methodology. Estimates by the group Iraq Body Count were the lowest, with its figures ranging from 88,851 to 96,976 civilians having died by September 30, 2008. In a survey for the World Health Organization, the Iraqi Health Ministry found 151,000 violent deaths out of 400,000 excess deaths beyond natural losses by June 2006. The highest figure came from the Opinion Research Business, which estimated that from 946,000 to 1,120,000 Iraqis had died by August 2007. The Lancet Survey estimated 601,027 violent deaths out of 654,965 excess deaths by June 2006. Of those deaths, 31 percent were attributed to the coalition, 24 percent to others, and 46 percent to unknown causes. More than half (56 percent) of the violent deaths were from gunshots, 13 percent from car bombs, 14 percent from other types of bombs, 13 percent from air strikes, 2 percent from accidents, and 2 percent from unknown causes.[7]

Nearly 4.7 million Iraqis—nearly one in five—fled their homes after the American invasion, with 2.5 million refugees relocating elsewhere within the country and another 2.2 million finding shelter in neighboring countries,

mostly in Syria and Jordan. Many women have been forced to turn to pros-
titution to survive; of the million refugees in Syria, perhaps as many as fifty
thousand women and girls are prostitutes. About 40 percent of the refugees
are Iraqi Christians. Perhaps the worst effect on Iraq's future viability has
been the "brain drain," with 40 percent of the members of Iraq's professional
class fleeing overseas, usually to developed countries.[8]

Most women in Iraq itself are certainly worse off now that Saddam's secular regime has been replaced by Islamist or tribal rule across much of the
country. Hundreds of women have been murdered in so-called "honor
killings" for violating tribal or Islamist mores. Beheadings, stonings, rapes,
genital mutilation, beatings, burnings, abductions, trafficking, and child
abuse are all on the rise.[9]

Iraq's health crisis is exacerbated by the devastation of the country's health
care system. Since the American invasion, more than 12,000 of Iraq's 34,000
doctors escaped to foreign exile, 2,000 were murdered, and 250 were kidnapped, one-third of the hospital beds were eliminated, and all institutions
suffer from critical shortages of medical equipment, medicine, and staff.

Finally there is the yearly bill for American taxpayers. When George W.
Bush and his fellow conservatives left office, their Iraq crusade scorecard
made very grim reading. Over $800 billion in American taxpayer dollars
had been expended in Iraq, with the monthly bill exceeding $12 billion—
$5,000 per second—for 2008. Sustaining one soldier for a year in Iraq costs
taxpayers $390,000. All of this may just be a down payment.

Most estimates of the Iraq War's financial costs to the United States are
deceptive because they do not include the indirect costs. By one calculation
the Iraq War's direct and indirect costs may reach a stunning $3.57 trillion
as capital is diverted from productive investments in the United States. The
most authoritative estimate to date comes from professors Joseph Stiglitz,
who won a Nobel prize for economics in 2001, and Linda Bilmes, a noted
economist. Using "conservative" and "moderate" criteria, they predicted that
the Iraq War would cost the United States at least $700 billion or $1.269
trillion, respectively, over ten years. The war's direct costs alone surpassed
the "conservative" figure in 2008, and they continue to soar.[10]

21

The Future of Iraq

Iraq's toll in lives and cash for the United States diminished as America's presence there slowly wound down. Meanwhile Tehran and Baghdad deepened their political, economic, and theological ties.

Prime Minister Nuri al-Maliki has often been derided as a weak leader, a multistranded rope in a tug-of-war among the Americans in the Green Zone, Moktada al-Sadr in Sadr City, Ayatollah Ali al-Sistani in Najaf, and Ayatollah Ali Khamenei in Tehran. Al-Maliki may be beholden to those and others, but he has used that weakness as a source of strength by playing them off against each other. His greatest source of power was fear—the fear of each major player that it will lose out to the others.

Al-Maliki's greatest coup was to force the Bush administration to formally accept a schedule for the withdrawal of American forces. The first step came on November 26, 2007, when he issued a statement of principles that called on the UN Security Council to return Iraq's sovereignty to the completely unrestricted status it held before August 1990. The Security Council complied by not extending the mandate for the United States to occupy Iraq beyond January 1, 2009. That in turn pressured the White House to cut a deal with al-Maliki over the future of American forces in Iraq. Talks opened in April 2008 and were concluded eight months later.

Under the agreement signed on November 19, 2008, the United States was to have ended all independent military operations by January 1, 2009, withdrawn from all "cities, towns, and villages" to designated remote desert bases by June 30, 2009, and withdrawn all troops from Iraq by December 31, 2011. Throughout that time American forces, contractors, and all other citizens would be subject to Iraqi law.

During the 2008 presidential campaign, President Barack Obama repeatedly pledged that he would end America's war in Iraq and withdraw the troops within sixteen months of entering the White House. Of 152,350 foreign troops in Iraq when Obama took office, 148,000 were American, 4,100 were British, and 250 from other countries.[1]

After taking the presidential oath, he spent more than a month speaking with experts. The result was a modification of his original plan. He extended the timetable by two months and agreed to leave a support force in Iraq for another year and a half. He announced his policy on February 27, 2009: "Let me say this as plainly as I can. By August 31, 2010, our combat mission in Iraq will end." Obama fulfilled his promise. He reduced the number of troops from 142,000 to below 50,000 by that date. The remaining troops are scheduled to be withdrawn by December 31, 2011.

Contrary to the criticisms of conservatives, Obama's policy was not a break with but a continuation and refinement of Bush's policy. The schedule was in perfect accord with the deal cut between President Bush and Prime Minister al-Maliki three months earlier.

But was that policy prudent? Whether or not the insurgency has been permanently suppressed remains to be seen. Ryan Crocker, America's ambassador to Iraq from March 2007 to February 2009, expressed the fears of many when he warned that "a precipitous withdrawal . . . could be very dangerous."[2] The worry was that pulling out American forces before the Iraqi army, paramilitary forces, and police were numerous and professional enough to maintain order could encourage the reeruption of civil war and insurgency.

Four vital factors made the descent of Iraq into another hell of insurgency and civil war less likely. Iraq's security forces were growing rapidly, from 250,000 in 2006 to 609,000 in 2008. All of this manpower should be able to smother any brushfires of violence. Meanwhile the religious frictions that might spark renewed bloodshed had just as steadily diminished. Another civil war was unlikely since years of fighting between Sunnis and Shiites had transformed Iraq from a religious and ethnic mosaic into a checkerboard. As

long as groups respect each other's turf, there would be no need for more violence. Nor did Al Qaeda pose a significant threat. It had thoroughly dis-
credited itself with indiscriminate bombings that had embittered most of the
Sunnis that it claimed to champion.

Iran is the fourth reason why another outbreak of war is unlikely. Thanks
to the conservative crusade, Iraq's fate largely rests in the hands of Iran. All
of the major Shiite leaders and groups have received money, guns, shelter,
and training from Iran. The Shiite-dominated government in Baghdad has
close ties with Tehran's, and they cooperate on many issues of mutual interest. The most important interest they share is to keep the peace and enjoy
the fruits of Shiite supremacy.

Iraq, however, is by no means an outright pawn of Iran. Virtually all
Iraqis are eager to restore Iraq's sovereignty, although they differ greatly on
just what to do with that power. The Sunnis obviously stand to lose the
most if the Shiites engage in a gratuitous payback for decades of repression.
The Kurds fear that the Shiites might try to rein in ever greater Kurdish
autonomy.

The relative health of Iraq's economy is a vital factor shaping whether
peace or violence will reign. The survivors in Iraq may well envy the
refugees, or even the dead. In 2010 the official jobless rate was at least 20
percent, with an additional 60 percent underemployed. Prices annually rose
by 50 percent. More than one in four children suffered from malnutrition.
Seven of ten Iraqis lacked access to clean and abundant water. Only four in
ten homes were connected to sewage systems. Over four million people
who fled their homes during the fighting must be resettled. Millions of Iraqis
lack adequate supplies of electricity, health clinics, and schools.

These socioeconomic conditions are likely to worsen. Iraq faces daunting
socioeconomic and political challenges in the years ahead. Nearly half of
Iraq's 24 million people are less than eighteen years old. That population
bulge is a crippling burden on Iraq's prospects for development. As they
grow into adulthood, these millions of young people will demand jobs,
goods, and services from an economy in which half the workforce is already
either jobless or underemployed. Economic reconstruction and diversification is essential for Iraq's future.

Diversification is, moreover, the key to economic development. By this

THE FUTURE OF IRAQ

measure alone, Iraq is an economic failure: oil exports accounts for 70 percent of the economy and 95 percent of government revenues. Petro-state economies and thus the regimes that control them depend on the market's whims for oil, as revenues soar and plummet with international oil prices.

Before the invasion, the Bush administration confidently predicted that Iraq's oil production would pay for the costs of occupation and reconstruction. It has not quite worked out that way. By early 2009 Iraq's oil production had yet to surpass its prewar level of 2.5 million barrels per day. The exact figure was a mystery. An Oil Ministry official admitted that "we do not know the exact quantity of oil we are exporting, nor the prices we are selling it for, and we do not know where the oil revenue is going."[3]

Oil revenues largely fuel the economy, which went into a tailspin as oil prices plunged from nearly $150 a barrel in the summer of 2008 to $40 a barrel a half year later, before creeping higher since then. This rollercoaster ride blew a huge hole in Iraq's revenues. For the foreseeable future, Iraq's development will have to be largely underwritten by international donors, with America shouldering most of the burden.

Yet another festering problem is the Awakening Councils. The surge was won more with dollars than bullets as the Americans paid off the local militias with money, arms, and training. In doing so they bought a short-term peace at the price of long-term tensions between the national security forces and the militias. Yet, these simmering tensions need not escalate into war if Baghdad respects Sunni sensitivities and keeps making the payments.

If a civil war does break out again, oil will most likely be the primary cause. The Kurds are transforming northern Iraq into an all but independent country. The Kurdistan Regional Government formally embraces three northern provinces, but Massoud Barzani, the governor, is leading efforts to spread Kurdish political, economic, and military influence over three adjacent provinces. With their own army, known as the Pesh Merga, the Kurds have the guns to back up that ambition. But their growing power is provoking worsening relations with Baghdad.

The biggest prize is the oil fields around Kirkuk. For a couple of decades Saddam Hussein had waged ethnic war against the Kurds by trying to drive them away and replace them with Arabs. Now the Kurds are trying to retake Kirkuk and drive out the Arabs and Turks. Provincial elections in Kirkuk scheduled for October 2008 were canceled when the Kurds, Turks, and Arabs failed to agree on how to divvy up the political spoils.[4]

If another insurgency or civil war does break out, can Iraq's security forces smother it? By November 2009 the paper strength of Iraq's army was 250,000, backed by an additional 145,000 paramilitary troops under the Interior Ministry, while the twenty-seven other ministries had their own security forces. The actual quality of those forces in conducting operations was generally rated from abysmal to not bad. In all, only 17 of 174 army battalions were deemed capable of conducting counterinsurgency missions.[5]

A largely paper-government presides over that largely paper-army. Conservatives boast that they destroyed Saddam Hussein's regime and replaced it with a popularly elected government with a constitution, bill of rights, and a process for regular, multi-party elections. Yet the substance of this achievement has been questioned. According to *Foreign Policy* magazine's "Failed States Index 2010," which uses a dozen social, economic, political, and military indicators to compare 177 countries, Iraq ranked as the seventh most unstable after Somalia, Chad, Sudan, Zimbabwe, the Congo, and Afghanistan. Thus the Bush team may have failed at state-building nearly as badly at it failed at nation-building.

Nonetheless, Iraq's government is by no means toothless. Prime Minister al-Maliki displayed ever more independence from Washington, if not from Tehran. With time Baghdad intends to transform Iraq's relationship with the United States from a client to a partner. The simultaneous drawing down of American forces and buildup of Iraqi forces gives the government additional wiggle-room. For instance, in February 2009 al-Maliki dismissed Vice President Joe Biden's remark that Washington needed to be "more aggressive" in forcing the Iraqi factions to work together, with the statement "The time for putting pressure on Iraq is over." But rather than turn to Tehran for reassurance, al-Maliki instead welcomed French president Nicolas Sarkozy, with his promises of aid and hopes to win contracts for French firms.[6]

The conservative crusade in Iraq was an enormously reckless gamble, the full results of which will not be known for years, if not decades. George W. Bush and his fellow conservatives promised that "victory" would usher in a new age of peace, prosperity, and democracy not just for Iraq, but eventually across the entire Middle East. In the president's vision "a liberated Iraq can show the power of freedom to transform that vital region by bringing hope and progress into the lives of millions. America's interest in security and America's belief in liberty both lead in the same direction—to a free and peaceful Iraq."[7] No doubt if Iraq is transformed from a thuggish anti-Western dictatorship into a pro-Western democracy, the Middle East's power balance and spectrum of political orientations will be sharply altered. But that is a huge "if."

So far history has revealed that conservative vision to be an utterly naive delusion. While the ability to destroy Saddam's regime was never in doubt, the political future for Iraq, and thus the region, is increasingly dire. The Bush team failed to be as capable at building as it was at destroying. "Nation-building" is a revolutionary challenge. The transformation of a country from despotism and poverty into democracy and prosperity demands uprooting and replacing not just institutions and peoples, but the very culture in which they live. Bush and his fellow conservatives truly believed that they could impose democracy on a poverty-stricken people torn by ethnic and religious hatreds checked only by a brutal dictatorship.

The insurgency reinforced the prewar warnings of the Cassandras that the Bush team's most likely legacy for a post-Saddam Iraq would be an anti-American, pro-Iranian regime rather than the Jeffersonian democracy promised by the conservatives. Iraq has indeed become the world's best training ground for terrorists to perfect their skills at fund-raising, organization, covert operations, and murder.[8]

The disastrous impact of the failed conservative crusade in Iraq goes far beyond that devastated country. The revolutionary impact of the Iraq War on the Middle East is comparable to Napoleon's invasion of Egypt in 1799, the collapse of the Ottoman Empire in 1918, Israel's foundation in 1948, and the Six Day War in 1967. Virtually all Arabs saw the American invasion as the latest version of Western imperialism, going back to the crusades that lasted from 1094 to 1291. The Iraq War inspired not democracy, but fanned the flames of Islamic radicalism and anti-Americanism throughout the Middle East. Iran and the Shiite and Sunni versions of Islamism are the Iraq War's most obvious immediate beneficiaries.

The conservative crusade became a giant self-fulfilling prophecy as it created what the Bush team claimed was the war's justification. Before March

2003 Iraq was not the launching pad for terrorist plots, let alone attacks against America. The triple containment policy from August 1990 until March 2003 was a great success—the United States contained Saddam, and Saddam contained Islamism, Iran, and terrorism. When the Bush team destroyed Saddam, they uncaged Islamism within Iraq and transformed that country into a battleground of Sunni against Shiite, Arab against Kurd, clan against clan, tribe against tribe, and ultimately into a breeding ground for an insurgency against the occupiers as well as a magnet for countless enraged young men from all around the world determined to kill Americans and their collaborators.

Will the conservative dream of democracy in the Middle East be realized? Most analysts are pessimistic. Rather than the "domino effect" envisioned by the conservatives, whereby a democratic Iraq will inspire democratic revolutions across the Middle East and beyond, the result may well be Islamist revolutions destroying pro-Western governments from Pakistan to Morocco. In 2011 mass demonstrations and violence erupted in Tunisia, Egypt, Bahrain, Libya, Jordan, and Yemen. How much of that was related to the conservative crusade in Iraq is impossible to determine. So far none of those political convulsions has resulted in either a liberal or an Islamist revolution.

The future of the Iraq experiment is just as uncertain. Brent Scowcroft, Bush senior's national security adviser, was "a skeptic about the ability to transform Iraq into a democracy in a reasonable period of time." He then warned: "What's going to happen the first time we hold an election in Iraq and it turns out the radicals win?"[9] Will conservatives be forever haunted by the question "Who lost Iraq?"

22

Excuses and Reasons

Of the array of charges against the Bush administration, the worst is that it lied to get the United States to go to war against a country that posed absolutely no threat. The result was to squander thousands of American lives, a couple of trillion dollars of wealth, and priceless honor for a war that actually empowered America's enemies.

The Bush team's justifications for the war jumped from one rationalization to another in the months leading up to the conflict. The conservatives asserted new accusations against Saddam when their previous accusations were exposed by experts as spurious or exaggerated. The threat of WMDs gave way to Saddam's sponsorship of terrorism, which then yielded to a crusade to end his evil rule and transform Iraq into a model of democracy, prosperity, and peace that would inspire similar revolutions across the Middle East and beyond.

Lacking a hard case, the conservatives typically raised the shrillness and spectrum of their accusations against both Iraq and anyone who opposed them. That strategy was as successful as it was disreputable. The louder and more often they broadcasted their claims, the more they drowned out the measured voices of realists and humanitarians who opposed the war, and the more their ranks swelled with those who blindly believed them.

Conservatives persist in angrily denouncing those who critique their version of "history." They insist that there is a deeper truth that exists beyond the mere facts that all good and true Americans would ultimately understand. That truth justified a crusade in which Iraq would be the kingpin struck down in a glorious series of wars that would eventually destroy all evil regimes.

Yet, in the end, none of these excuses mattered. Most Americans either fell for or could not have cared less about the Bush team's "bait and switch" excuses for the war. The average American was filled with rage and fear not just for September 11, but for an array of real and imagined threats and signs of American impotence.

While many professionals in the intelligence community may have shared that rage and fear, they harbored no illusions about who had attacked the United States on September 11. They were outraged that the administration had pressured them to write reports that skewed the evidence, which the conservatives then cherry-picked and warped to justify their war. When even those blatant distortions proved to be too flimsy, Defense Secretary Rumsfeld assigned his deputy Paul Wolfowitz and under secretary Douglas Feith to form a "B Team"—their Office of Special Plans—that would shift through the mountains of information to find any overlooked "nuggets" for their case. The trouble was that nearly everything they found was fool's gold. That, of course, did not stop the Bush team from peddling it as "evidence" that Iraq had WMDs and ties to Al Qaeda and September 11.[1]

The most notorious known abuse of intelligence was the Bush team's claim that Iraq had sought enriched uranium from Niger despite the CIA's explanation that this rumor was not true. As if repeatedly telling a lie that would then be used as an excuse for an unnecessary war was not heinous enough, the Bush team was ruthless toward the former ambassador who investigated the rumor, and his wife. Wilson exposed the background to the lie in an article entitled, "What I Did Not Find in Africa," which was published in the *New York Times* on July 6, 2003.[2]

The Bush administration responded by leaking word that Joseph Wilson's wife, Valerie Plame, was a covert CIA officer. That revelation not only ruined Plame's career but potentially endangered the lives of any foreigners with whom she had associated during her two decades undercover and would have a chilling effect on other foreigners whom the CIA would try to recruit—a potential disaster for American national security. It is for these reasons that exposing the names of CIA officers is a felony. The Bush administration had two motives in "outing" Valerie Plame: vengeance against a whistle-blower and intimidation against any other insiders who were tempted to reveal the truth.[3]

How badly did the Bush administration corrupt or warp the intelligence used to justify the Iraq War? On February 7, 2004, the president announced that he would form a seven-member bipartisan panel to investigate any shortcomings in the intelligence community over the analysis of Iraq. The panel would not present its findings until March 2005, long after Bush's bid for reelection was decided.

That cynical parade of contrived excuses to justify the Iraq War got downright bizarre in a meeting between Bush and journalist Bob Woodward, who was writing a book on the Iraq War. When Woodward said that the search for WMDs would be a vital part of the story, Bush replied, "What's this got to do with it?" Later at a press conference when Bush was asked how he could justify all the distortions that he and his administration wielded to scare the nation to war, he offered the Orwellian retort that it was his critics who were engaging in "revisionist history." Being trapped in his lies outraged him. "So what's the difference?" Bush demanded when Diane Sawyer of ABC News pointed out that after nine months the investigators had found no WMDs in Iraq.[4]

So if the stated reasons for the Bush administration's decision to wage war against Iraq were false, what were the real reasons? Ideology, politics, psychology, and profits all played complex interrelated roles.

Politically the Bush team believed that the Iraq War could boost not just the president's chance for reelection, but also expand Republican domination of the federal, state, and local governments in the next election. Not surprisingly, polls consistently revealed that most Americans believed that the Iraq War was just even if no WMDs or links with Al Qaeda were found. By November 2, 2004, that support had declined from an initial two-thirds to half. That, however, was enough to reelect George W. Bush with 51 percent of the vote.

As for profit, economics and politics are inseparable. While the war would distort and stunt the economy over the long run as the national debt soared, it was a short-term windfall for Bush and the Republican Party. By funneling tens of billions of dollars in reconstruction contracts into the coffers of its corporate allies, the Republican Party reaped in grateful return hundreds of millions of dollars in campaign contributions.

And then there is ideology. Unilaterally warring against Iraq in defiance of international law, morality, and opinion represents one of conservatism's greatest triumphs to date. Designating and destroying "bad guys" is essential to letting the "good guys" justify their entire ideological agenda whose core is a spoils system of crony capitalism and massive tax cuts for the rich.

But the conservative crusade in Iraq was as much about psychology as ideology, profits, and politics.[5] Several psychological studies of George W. Bush argued that by destroying Saddam's regime, he could at once correct his father's mistakes (according to conservatives), and surpass his achievements. Yet the psychoanalysts point to a vital underlying reason for the war far beyond Bush junior's Oedipus complex. There is a perverse psychology for those too cowardly to fight in wars that they otherwise wildly cheer. Perhaps to compensate for the deep flaws in their own character, they tend to project onto scapegoats their own self-loathing and beat the drum for war the loudest. Starting with George W. Bush himself, the conservative ranks are filled with those who dodged the draft and possible Vietnam combat. Those few Republicans in the White House and Congress who did serve in Vietnam, such as Colin Powell, John McCain, and Chuck Hagel, were the most skeptical about the Bush team's exhilarating rush to war against Iraq.

In the end, perhaps the most fundamental reason for the Iraq War was rooted in a perverse circular logic. Power is the ability to get others to do what they would otherwise rather not do. At times power is asserted by pure rational or emotional persuasion. More often than not, persuasion is backed by coercion; a state demands that another state change its behavior "or else." Coercion works if one state believes the other state has both the will and appropriate force to act on its threats. Ideally a reputation for power is enough to get others to submit without the use of force, which in turn enhances that stated reputation for power.

Thus, after months of table-pounding bluster, the Bush team would have weakened their credibility had they appeared to back off. Indeed, George W. Bush ordered the invasion of Iraq even though Saddam Hussein had signaled he was willing to give in to virtually all of the White House and

UN demands. By its own admission, the Bush administration hoped that the Iraq War would have a "demonstration effect" by which in the future other states would swiftly submit to, rather than defy, White House demands.

In reality, the conservative crusade smashed the bottle containing Islamism within and beyond Iraq, which Saddam had so brutally maintained. Iran and the Shiite version of Islamism were the most immediate victors. What we will most likely witness is one Islamist revolution after another besieging and most likely toppling one erstwhile "friendly" government after another across the Muslim world, most disastrously in Pakistan. And because of that, the United States will likely be compelled to expend trillions of dollars and tens of thousands of lives trying to battle these Islamist revolutions to preserve American security. In all, the conservative crusade in Iraq and Muslim world will be ever more devastating to American power, wealth, security, and honor.

Notes

INTRODUCTION

1 Timothy Williams and Rod Nordland, "Former Premier Wins Narrowly in Iraq Election," *New York Times* (*NYT* hereafter), May 27, 2010.

2 "Names of the Dead," *NYT*, March 20, 2010; Linda Bilmes and Joseph Stiglitz, *The Three Trillion Dollar War: The True Cost of the Iraq Conflict* (New York: Norton, 2008), 2–3.

3 The Pew Research Center for the People and the Press, Pew Institute Global Attitudes Survey, various years, http://people-press.org.

4 Civilian Deaths from Violence, Iraq Body Count, Iraqbodycount.org; Pew Institute Global Attitudes Survey, various years, http://people-press.org.

5 Kai Hafez, "The Iraq War 2003 in Western Media and Public Opinion: Case Study on the Effects of Military (Non-)Involvement on Conflict Perceptions," *Global Media Journal* 3, no. 5 (Fall 2004); Adam Nagourney and Janet Alder, "Threats and Responses: The Polls," *NYT*, March 11, 2003; Megan Thee, "Support for the Initial Invasion Has Risen," *NYT*, July 24, 2007.

6 F. Christian Miller, *Blood Money: A Story of Wasted Billions, Lost Lives, and Corporate Greed in Iraq* (New York: Little, Brown, 2006).

CHAPTER 1: THE LEGACY

1 For an argument that casts doubt on the seriousness of the plot, see Seymour Hersh, "Did Iraq Try to Assassinate Ex-President Bush in 1993," in Micah L. Sifry and Christopher Cerf, eds., *The Iraq War Reader: History, Documents, Opinions* (New York: Simon & Schuster), 140–61.

2 Karen DeYoung and Walter Pincus, "Despite Heated Rhetoric, Bush Policy on Iraq Follows Clinton Script," *International Herald Tribune* (*IHT* hereafter), January 25, 2002.

CHAPTER 2: THWARTED DREAMS

1   Ron Suskind, *The Price of Loyalty: George W. Bush, the White House, and the Education of Paul O'Neill* (New York: Simon & Schuster, 2004), 34; Elaine Sciolino and Alison Mitchell, "Calls for New Push into Iraq Gain Power in Washington," *NYT*, December 3, 2001.

2   Massimo Calabresi, "Where's Colin Powell," *Time*, September 10, 2001; Robin Wright, "Bush Team Is Divided on Policy toward Iraq," *IHT*, February 15, 2001; DeYoung and Pincus, "Despite Heated Rhetoric."

3   Sciolino and Mitchell, "Calls for New Push into Iraq."

4   Thom Shanker, "Iraqi Opposition Ready to Broadcast Satellite TV Program Financed by U.S.," *NYT*, August 28, 2001; DeYoung and Pincus, "Despite Heated Rhetoric."

5   Thom Shanker, "Rumsfeld Says Iraq has Improved Air Defenses since February," *NYT*, August 4, 2001.

6   Charles Babington, "Iraqi Sites Attacked in Raid by U.S. and Britain," *IHT*, February 17, 2001.

7   Mike Allen, "Bush's Brevity: The Soul of What?" *IHT*, February 20, 2001.

8   Neela Banerjee, "Stable World Oil Prices Are Likely to Become a War Casualty, Experts Say," *NYT*, October 2, 2002.

9   Neil MacFarquhar, "Iraq Halts Petroleum Exports to Put Pressure on the Americans," *NYT*, April 9, 2002.

10   Alan Sipress, "Powell, to Bolster Iraq Embargo, Wants to Close Off Syrian Leak," *IHT*, February 19, 2001.

11   Colum Lynch, "Russia Emerges as Top Customer for Iraqi Exports," *IHT*, January 17, 2002.

12   John Tagliabue, "Europeans Strive to Tighten Trade Ties with Iraq," *NYT*, September 19, 2002.

CHAPTER 3: COOKING THE BOOKS

1   Richard Clarke, *Against All Enemies: Inside America's War on Terrorism* (New York: Free Press, 2002), 32.

2   Clarke, *Against All Enemies*, 30; George Tenet, *The Center of the Storm: My Years at the CIA* (New York: HarperCollins, 2007), 302–19.

3   Elaine Sciolino and Patrick Tyler, "Some Pentagon Officials and Advisors Seek to Oust Iraq's Leader in War's Next Phase," *NYT*, October 12, 2001; Judith Miller, "Former Terrorism Official Faults White House on 9/11," *NYT*, March 22, 2004; "Excerpts from the President's Remarks on the War on Terrorism," *NYT*, October 12, 2001.

4   Patrick Tyler and John Tagliabue, "Czechs Confirm Iraqi Agent Met with Terror Ringleader," *NYT*, October 27, 2001; Chris Hedges and Donald McNeil, "New Clue Fails to Explain Iraq Role in September 11 Attack," *NYT*, December 16, 2001; *The 9/11 Commission Report: The Final Report of the National Commission on Terrorist Attacks Upon the United States* (New York: W. W. Norton, 2004), 228–29.

5   Elisabeth Bumiller, "Readmit Inspectors, President Tells Iraq; 'Or Else' Is Unstated," *NYT*, November 27, 2001; Bob Woodward, *State of Denial: Bush at War, Part III* (New York: Simon & Schuster), 81.

6   Sarah Lyall, "In Oslo Annan Warns U.S. against Striking Iraq," *NYT*, December 10, 2001; Sarah Lyall, "Iraq Urged to Allow Inspectors," *NYT*, December 20, 2001.

7 Steven Erlanger, "Britain Presses U.S. for Nation Building in Afghanistan," *NYT*, October 12, 2001.

8 Todd Purham, "Top Republicans Break with Bush on Iraq Strategy," *NYT*, August 16, 2002; Eric Schmitt, "Iraq Is Defiant as G.O.P. Leader Opposes Attack," *NYT*, August 9, 2002.

9 Tenet, *My Years at the CIA*, 315.

10 Bob Woodward, *Bush at War* (New York: Simon & Schuster, 2003), 333.

11 Neil Lewis and David Sanger, "Bush May Request Congress's Backing on Iraq, Aides Say," *NYT*, August 28, 2002.

12 David Manning, "The Secret Downing Street Memo," *Times* (London), May 1, 2005; Walter Pincus, "British Intelligence Warned of Iraq War," *Washington Post*, May 13, 2005.

13 Tenet, *My Years at the CIA*, 348.

14 Douglas Jehl, "Qaeda-Iraq Link U.S. Cited Is Tied to Coercion Claim," *NYT*, December 9, 2005; Scott Shane, "Iraqi Official Paid by C.I.A. Gave Account of Weapons," *NYT*, March 22, 2006.

15 Douglas Jehl, "Report Says White House Ignored C.I.A. on Iraq Chaos," *NYT*, October 13, 2005.

16 Joseph Wilson, "What I Did Not Find in Niger," *NYT*, July 6, 2003.

17 Ron Suskind, *The Way of the World: A Story of Truth and Hope in an Age of Extremism* (New York: Harper, 2008).

18 James Risen and David Johnson, "Efforts to Show Iraq-Qaeda Link Cause Friction within FBI and CIA," *IHT*, February 3, 2003; Greg Myre, "War with Iraq Serves as Wedge in Mideast," *IHT*, March 21, 2004; Hersh, "Did Iraq Try to Assassinate," 140–61.

19 *The 9/11 Commission Report.* See also Tenet, *My Years at the CIA*, 341–58; Yousef Bodansky, *Bin Laden: The Man Who Declared War on America* (New York: Prima, 2001), 232–25, 344–47, 361–62.

20 William J. Broad and David Johnston, "U.S. Inquiry Tried, but Failed, to Link Iraq to Anthrax Attack," *NYT*, December 22, 2001.

CHAPTER 4: THE BLANK CHECK

1 "Full Text: In Cheney's Words," *NYT*, August 26, 2002; "Bush's Speech to U.N.," *NYT*, September 12, 2002; White House Archives, September 15, 2006, http://georgewbush-whitehouse.archives; Thom Shanker and David Sanger, "Threats and Responses: Strategy, Rumsfeld Says other Nations Promise to Aid Attack on Iraq," *NYT*, September 19, 2002; Jeffrey Richelson, "Iraq and Weapons of Mass Destruction," *National Security Briefing Books* no. 80, February 11, 2004.

2 "On United States Involvement in Iraq," *NYT*, September 6, 2002.

3 "In Bush's Words: On Iraq, U.N. Must Face Up to Founding Purposing," *NYT*, September 12, 2002.

4 Julia Preston and Todd Purdum, "Threats and Responses: Diplomacy, U.N. Inspectors Can Return Unconditionally, Iraq Says," *NYT*, September 17, 2002.

5 Elisabeth Bumiller, "President to Seek Congress's Assent Over Iraq Action," *NYT*, September 5, 2002; David Firestone and David Sanger, "Congress Now Promises to Hold Weeks of Hearings About Iraq," *NYT*, September 6, 2002.

6 Patrick Tyler, "Britain's Case: Iraqi Program to Amass Is 'Up and Running,'" *NYT*, September 25, 2002; Warren Hoge, "Weapons Development Called Iraq's Priority," *NYT*, September 10, 2002.

7 Thomas Friedman on *Charlie Rose Show*, PBS, April 9, 2002.

8 "Americans on Iraq and the Economy," *NYT*, October 7, 2002; Data Resource Center, CBS/New York Times Poll, "Terrorism and Preparedness," October 2002, http://dx.doi.org/10.3886/ICPSR03706.

9 "Transcript: Confronting the Iraqi Threat 'Is Crucial to Winning the War on Terrorism,'" *NYT*, October 8, 2002.

10 "C.I.A. Letter to Senate on Baghdad's Intentions," *NYT*, October 9, 2002; Michael Gordon, "U.S. Aides Split on Assessment of Iraq's Plans," *NYT*, October 10, 2002; Tenet, *My Years at the CIA*, 321–39, 341–58.

11 "Resolution that Congress Approved the Right to Use Force in Iraq," *NYT*, October 11, 2002.

CHAPTER 5: THE INSPECTIONS

1 Joseph Fitchett, "In UN Report, Ammunition for Two Sides," *IHT*, January 28, 2003; Timothy O'Brien, "Cooperation Falls Short, Blix Says," *IHT*, January 28, 2003; Michael Gordon and James Risen, "Nuclear Report on Iraq Challenges U.S. Rationale," *IHT*, March 29, 2003. For the best overall account of the inspections, see Hans Blix, *Disarming Iraq* (New York: Pantheon, 2004).

2 "Deadly Comparisons: The Open Questions about Iraq's Weapons Program," *NYT*, December 13, 2002.

3 "Deadly Comparisons."

4 Judith Miller and Julia Preston, "From Blix, a Challenge to the U.S. Use of Report," *IHT*, February 1, 2003.

5 Patrick Tyler, "Goal of Saddam," *IHT*, January 20, 2003.

6 Brian Knowlton, "Bush's Timetable: A Matter of Weeks," *IHT*, January 31, 2003; Bob Woodward, *Plan of Attack* (New York: Simon & Schuster), 224; Woodward, *State of Denial*, 106.

7 Steven Weisman, "Stunning Setback for U.S. Resulted from Series of Mistakes," *IHT*, March 18, 2003.

CHAPTER 6: THE SECOND RESOLUTION

1 Weisman, "Stunning Setback."

2 Patrick Tyler, "Intelligence Break Lets Powell Link Iraq and Qaeda," *NYT*, *IHT*, February 7, 2003; Christopher Marquis, "No 'Smoking Gun' Found in Iraq, Powell Admits," *IHT*, January 9, 2004.

CHAPTER 7: THE SEARCH FOR ALLIES

1 Peter Brooke, "Patten Assails 'Unilateralist' U.S.," *IHT*, February 16, 2002.

2 Steven Erlanger, "U.S. Quietly Chides German for His Dissension on Iraq," *NYT*, August 17, 2002.

3 Thomas Fuller, "American Lobbyists Swayed Eastern Europe's Iraq Response," *IHT*, February 20, 2003.

4 Craig Smith, "East Europe Refutes Chirac," *IHT*, February 19, 2003.

5 Joseph Fitchett, "Allies Face a Fresh Crisis," *IHT*, February 10, 2003.

6 Warren Hoe, "Blair Defends Iraq Policy as U.K. Skepticism Rises," *IHT*, January 14, 2003.

7 Joel Brinkley, "Turkey's No Frustrates War Aims," *IHT*, March 3, 2003.

8 Michael Gordon, "U.S. Is Preparing Bases in Gulf States to Run Iraq War," *NYT*, December 2, 2002.

9 Susan Sachs, "Arab Push to Get Saddam to Disarm Fails in Disarray," *IHT*, March 14, 2002.

10 C. J. Chivers, "Kurds Ask U.S. to Bar Turks," *IHT*, February 27, 2003.

11 Douglas Jehl, "Agency Belittles Information Given by Iraqi Defectors," *NYT*, September 29, 2003.

12 Craig Smith, "Hussein Foes Meet in London but Rivalries Fracture Unity," *NYT*, December 14, 2002; Craig Smith, "Meeting of Iraqi Opposition Seeks to Bar U.S. Dominance," *NYT*, December 15, 2002; Craig Smith, "Groups Outline Plans for Governing a Post-Hussein Iraq," *NYT*, December 18, 2002.

CHAPTER 8: CHEERLEADERS AND DISSIDENTS

1 Jim Kuypers, *Bush's War: Media Bias and Justifications for War in a Terrorist Age* (Lanham, MD: Rowman & Littlefield, 2006); Ian S. Lustick, *Trapped in the War on Terror* (Philadelphia: University of Pennsylvania Press, 2006).

2 For an overview on this and other polls, see "Iraq: The War Card," The Center for Public Integrity, 2008, http://projects.publicintegrity.org/war card charts/polls.

3 John Kerry Speech at Georgetown University, January 23, 2003, JohnKerry.com.

4 Nicholas Kristof, "Containment Is Better," *IHT*, February 9, 2003.

5 Frank Bruni, "Pope Calls Potential War in Iraq a Defeat for Humanity," *IHT*, January 14, 2003; Laurie Goodstein, "War on Iraq Not Yet Justified, Bishops Say," *NYT*, November 13, 2002.

6 William Broad, "41 Nobelists Caution on a Preventive War," *IHT*, January 29, 2003.

7 Steven Greenhouse, "U.S. Labor Groups Break Tradition and Criticize Bush Policy," *IHT*, March 3, 2003.

8 Felicity Barringer, "U.S. Diplomat Resigns to Protest Iraq Policy," *IHT*, February 28, 2003.

9 James Risen, "Iraq Said To Have Tried To Reach Last Minute Deal To Avert War," *NYT*, November 6, 2003.

10 For perhaps the best comprehensive and succinct realist view, see John J. Mearsheimer and Stephen M. Walt, "An Unnecessary War," *Foreign Policy* no. 134 (January–February 2003): 50–59.

11 George A. Lopez and David Cortright, "Containing Iraq: Sanctions Worked," *Foreign Affairs* 83, no. 4 (July–August 2004): 97–98, 90–103.

12 Brent Scowcroft, "Don't Attack Iraq," *Wall Street Journal*, August 25, 2002.

13 Conrad C. Crane and W. Andrew Terrill, *Reconstructing Iraq: Insights, Challenges, and Missions for Military Forces in a Post-Conflict Scenario* (Carlisle, PA: Strategic Studies Institute, 2003), 18–19.

14 Kenneth Pollack, *The Threatening Storm: The Case for Invading Iraq* (New York: Random House, 2002).

CHAPTER 9: PLANNING "SHOCK AND AWE"

1 Joel Brinkley, "No Pause in War, U.S. Says," *IHT*, March 31, 2003.

2 Michael Gordon, "U.S. Air Raids in 2002 Prepared for War with Iraq," *NYT*, July 19, 2003; Douglas Jehl with Dexter Filkins, "U.S. Moved to Undermine Iraqi Before War with Iraq," *NYT*, August 10, 2002.

3 Tenet, *My Years at the CIA*, 355–97.

4 Thom Shanker and Eric Schmitt, "Cyber-warfare in Iraq Already Has Broken Out," *IHT*, February 24, 2003.

CHAPTER 10: UNLEASHING "SHOCK AND AWE"

1 Marjorie Connelly, "Most Americans Approve of War on Iraq," *IHT*, March 22, 2003.

2 John Broder, "A Nation at War: The Commander, Doha Qatar, Franks Describes a War 'Unlike Any in History,'" *NYT*, March 23, 2003.

3 Gordon, "U.S. Air Raids in 2002."

4 Joel Brinkley, "As Some Wells Burn, Iraq Is Warned Not to Ruin Oil Riches," *IHT*, March 21, 2003.

5 Anthony Cordesman, "The Pentagon's Scariest Thoughts," *IHT*, March 22, 2003; Scott Ritter, *The War on Iraq: What Team Bush Doesn't Want You to Know* (New York: Context Books, 2003).

6 David Sanger and John Burns, "Anti-aircraft Batteries Open Up in Baghdad," *IHT*, March 20, 2003.

7 David Sanger, "In Washington, Rumblings of Doubt About the War's Progress," *IHT*, March 31, 2003; Brinkley, "No Pause in War."

8 Sanger, "In Washington, Rumblings of Doubt"; Joseph Hoar, "Why Aren't There Enough Troops in Iraq?" *NYT*, April 2, 2003; Thom Shanker and John Tierney, "Top Ranked Officer Denounces Critics of Iraq Campaign," *NYT*, April 2, 2003.

9 Jim Ruthenberg, "Ex-Generals Defend Their Blunt Comments," *NYT*, April 2, 2003.

10 Barry James, "U.S. Global Effort to Shut Iraqi Efforts Meets Refusals," *IHT*, March 22, 2003; Barry James, "Jordan and Italy Expel Iraq Envoys; Vatican Demurs," *IHT*, March 24, 2003; "UN Rights Body Rejects Request for Meeting on Iraq," *IHT*, March 28, 2003.

11 Brian Knowlton, "Bush and Putin Argue over Iraqi Sales and Aid," *IHT*, March 25, 2003; Joel Brinkley, "Rumsfeld Assails Syrian Aid to Iraq," *IHT*, March 29, 2003; C. J. Chivers, "An Iranian-Backed Brigade Sets Up Camp in Northern Iraq," *IHT*, March 4, 2003.

12 Charlie LeDuff with David Rodhe, "Turkey Backs Off on Iraq Incursion," *IHT*, March 27, 2003; Steven Weisman, "Powell Patches Things Up as Turkey Consents to Help," *NYT*, February 15, 2003.

13 Mark Landler, "French and German Business Wary of Backlash," *IHT*, March 28, 2003; Barry James, "Congressmen Urge U.S. Boycott of Paris Air Show," *IHT*, February 15, 2003.

14 Alan Cowell, "Kind Words from France (So to Speak)," *IHT*, March 28, 2003.

CHAPTER 11: PICKING UP THE PIECES

1 "Pentagon: Some Explosives Possibly Destroyed," Associated Press, October 29, 2004.

2 Dexter Filkins, "Mobs Ransack Homes and Set Fire to Government Sites," *NYT*, April 12, 2003; Scott Ritter, " Weapons Caches We'll Never See," *NYT*, August 25, 2004; Matthew Bogdanos, "Fighting for Iraq's Culture," *IHT*, March 6, 2003.

3   Tenet, *My Years at the CIA*, 317–18, 426.

4   Jane Perlez, "Pentagon and State Departments in Tug-of-War over Aid Disbursal," *NYT*, April 1, 2003; Eric Schmitt and Joel Brinkley, "State Department Study Foresaw Trouble Now Plaguing Iraq," *NYT*, October 19, 2003; David Rieff, "Blueprint for a Mess: How the Bush Administration's Prewar Planning Bungled Postwar Iraq," *New York Times Magazine*, November 2, 2003; Frederick M. Burkle, Bradley A. Woodruff, and Eric K. Noji, "Lessons and Controversies: Planning and Immediate Relief in the Aftermath of the War in Iraq," *Third World Quarterly* 26, no. 4/5 (2005): 797–814.

5   *Human Development Report*, U.N. Development Program, 2005, http://hdr.undp.org/en/.

6   For a good summary of Garner and ORHA, see Woodward, *State of Denial*, 111–89.

7   George Packer, *The Assassin's Gate: America in Iraq* (New York: Farrar, Straus & Giroux, 2006), 180–95; Woodward, *State of Denial*, 190–212.

8   Tenet, *My Years at the CIA*, 422–23.

CHAPTER 12: PASSING THE HAT

1   Eric Schmitt, "Washington Squabbling over Who Says What the War Would Cost," *IHT*, March 1, 2003; Brian Knowlton, "Citing Good Progress Bush Urges Quick Approval of Funds," *IHT*, March 26, 2003; David Firestone and Eric Lichtblau, "Panels Approve War Spending but Reject Free Rein for White House," *NYT*, April 2, 2003; David Firestone, "House and Senate Approve Bush's Wartime Spending Request," *NYT*, April 4, 2003.

2   Paul Wolfowitz, "Words on the Cost: Paul Wolfowitz," *NYT*, September 10, 2003.

3   Richard Oppel, "New Trade Bank to Extend Credit for Rebuilding," *NYT*, July 22, 2003.

4   Elizabeth Becker, "Help Is Tied to Approval by the U.N.," *NYT*, April 1, 2003; Felicity Barringer, "Billions in Aid from the U.N. Is in Limbo Official Says," *NYT*, April 22, 2003.

5   Sarah Kershaw, "Iraq's Neighbors Issue Declaration Criticizing Lifting of Sanctions," *NYT*, April 20, 2003.

6   Felicity Barringer and Elisabeth Bumiller, "France Urging U.N. to Suspend Iraq Penalties," *NYT*, April 23, 2003.

7   Patrick Tyler, "U.N. Chef Issues Firestorm by Calling Iraq War 'Illegal,'" *NYT*, September 17, 2004.

8   Steven Weisman, "Over $13 Billion in Aid Is Pledged to Rebuild Iraq," *NYT*, October 25, 2003; Steven Weisman, "Funds for Iraq Falling Short of Pledges, Figures Show," *NYT*, December 7, 2003; Craig Smith, "France Says It Is Willing to Make Deal on Iraq's Foreign Debt," *NYT*, December 16, 2003; Steven Weisman, "U.S. Tackles Iraq Debts to Nations in Mideast," *IHT*, January 6, 2004; "Plan Cancels Some of the Debt Owed by Iraq," *NYT*, November 21, 2004.

CHAPTER 13: THAT ELUSIVE "SMOKING GUN"

1   Judith Miller, "A Chronicle of Confusion in the U.S. Hunt for Hussein's Chemical and Germ Weapons," *NYT*, July 20, 2003; James Risen and Judith Miller, "Officials Say Bush Seeks $600 million to Hunt Iraq Arms," *NYT*, October 2, 2003; "Inspector Faults Data on Iraq's Weapons," *IHT*, January 26, 2004; Brian Knowlton, "'We Were All Wrong,' Inspector Says," *IHT*, January 29, 2004; Woodward, *State of Denial*, 210–28, 242–43, 277–82.

2   Scott Ritter, *Frontier Justice: Weapons of Mass Destruction and the Bushwhacking of America* (New York: Context Books, 2003); Scott Ritter, "Not Everyone Got It Wrong on Iraq's Weapons," *IHT*, February 6, 2004; Blix, *Disarming Iraq*; Warren Hoge, "Ex-U.N. Inspector Has Harsh Words for Bush," *NYT*, March 16, 2004.

3   Scott Shane, "Iraqi Dictator Told of Fearing Iran More than He Did U.S.," *NYT*, July 3, 2009.

4   George W. Bush speech, May 1, 2003, "Lack of Hard Evidence of Iraqi Weapons: A Crucial Advance in the Campaign against Terror," guardian.co.uk.

CHAPTER 14: IMPOSING DEMOCRACY

1   George W. Bush speech, November 6, 2003.

2   Linda Robinson, *Tell Me How This Ends: General David Petraeus and the Search for a Way Out of Iraq* (New York: Public Affairs, 2008), 10.

3   Jeff Gerth and Scott Shane, "U.S. Is Said to Plant Articles in Iraq Newspapers," *NYT*, December 1, 2005; Eric Schmitt, "Military Admits Planting News in Iraq," *NYT*, December 4, 2005; Thom Shanker, "No Breach Is Seen in Planting U.S. Propaganda in Iraq Media," *NYT*, March 22, 2006; David Cloud, "U.S. Urged to Stop Paying Iraqi Reporters," *NYT*, May 24, 2006; George W. Bush speech, "Lack of Hard Evidence of Iraqi Weapons."

CHAPTER 15: THE SPOILS OF WAR

1   Douglas Jehl, "The Struggle for Iraq: The Reconstruction; Insiders' New Firm Consults on Iraq," *NYT*, September 30, 2003; Edmund Andrews, "Bush Got $500,000 from Companies that Got Contracts, Study Finds," *NYT*, October 31, 2003; Edmund Andrews and Neela Banerjee, "Companies Get a Few Days to Offer Bids on Iraq Work," *NYT*, October 19, 2003; "Private Security Contractors at War: Ending the Culture of Impunity," Human Rights First, January 15, 2008; Stuart Bowen, Special Inspector General for Iraq Reconstruction, Testimony before Congress, January 24, 2008; *Defense Contracting in Iraq: Issues and Options for Congress*, Congressional Research Service report for Congress, August 15, 2008; *Private Security Contractors in Iraq: Background, Legal Status, and Other Issues*, Congressional Research Service report for Congress, August 25, 2008.

2   Diana Henrique, "First Bids to Rebuild Iraq to Go Only to Americans," *IHT*, March 24, 2003; Douglas Jehl, "Pentagon Bars Three Nations from Iraq Bids," *NYT*, December 10, 2003; David Sanger and Douglas Jehl, "Bush Seeks Help of Allies Barred from Iraq Deals," *NYT*, December 11, 2003; Erin Arvedlund, "Allies Angered at Exclusion from Bidding," *NYT*, December 11, 2003; "U.S. Opens Contracts on Rebuilding Iraq," *IHT*, February 12, 2004.

3   Erick Eckholm, "White House Officials and Cheney Aide Approved Halliburton Contract in Iraq, Pentagon Says," *NYT*, June 14, 2004; Erick Eckholm, "A Top U.S. Contracting Official for the Army Calls for an Inquiry in the Halliburton Case," *NYT*, October 25, 2005.

4   Don Van Natta, "High Payments to Halliburton for Fuel in Iraq," *NYT*, December 20, 2003; Douglas Jehl, "U.S. Sees Evidence of Overcharging in Iraq Contracts," December 12, 2003; Erick Eckholm, "Auditors Testify About Waste in Iraq Contracts," *NYT*, June 16, 2004; Erick Eckholm, "Excess Fuel Billing by Halliburton in Iraq Is Put at $108 million in Audit," *NYT*, March 15, 2005; James Glanz, "Audit Describes Misuse of Funds in Iraq Projects," *NYT*, January 25, 2006; James Glanz, "Army to Pay Halliburton Unit Most Costs Disputed by Audit," *NYT*, February 27, 2006; James Glanz, "Report Adds to

Criticism of Halliburton's Iraq Role," *NYT*, March 29, 2006; Erick Eckholm, "Lawmakers, Including Republicans, Criticize Pentagon on Disputed Billing by Halliburton," *NYT*, June 27, 2006; James Glanz, "Idle Contractors Add Millions to Iraq Rebuilding," *NYT*, October 25, 2006; Scott Shane and Ron Nixon, "U.S. Contractors Becoming a Virtual Fourth Branch of Government," *NYT*, February 8, 2007.

5   David Sanger and Eric Schmitt, "White House Favorite Is Becoming Its Headache," *NYT*, April 27, 2003; Richard Oppel, "U.S. to Halt Payment to Iraqi Group Headed by a Onetime Pentagon Favorite," *NYT*, May 18, 2004; James Risen and David Johnston, "Chalabi Reportedly Told Iran that U.S. Had Code," *NYT*, June 2, 2004.

6   Richard May, "Wasting Money in Iraq," Center for Defense Information (CDI), April 12, 2007.

7   T. Christian Miller, "Private Contractors Outnumber U.S. Troops in Iraq," *Los Angeles Times*, July 4, 2007; "Wartime Use of Contractors," *IHT*, February 2, 2008.

8   Peter Grier, "Record Number of US Contractors in Iraq," *Christian Science Monitor*, August 18, 2008; Marion E. Bowman, "Privatizing While Transforming," *Defense Horizons* no. 57 (July 2007): 4.

9   *Contractors' Support of U.S. Operations in Iraq*, Congressional Budget Office paper, August 2008.

10 David Ivanovich, "Contractor Deaths Up 17 Percent Across Iraq in 2007," *Houston Chronicle*, February 9, 2008.

11 Eric Schmitt, "Afghan Arms Are at Risk, Report Says," *NYT*, February 12, 2009; James Glanz, "U.S. Failed to Oversee Corps on Iraq Work, Agency Says," *NYT*, January 30, 2008.

12 Richard Oppel, Diana Henriques, and Elizabeth Becker, "Who Will Put Iraq Back Together?" *NYT*, March 23, 2003.

CHAPTER 16: "BRING 'EM ON!"

1   Anthony Cordesman, *Iraq's Evolving Insurgency* (Washington, D.C.: Center for Strategic and International Studies, 2005); Dexter Filkins, "Profusion of Rebel Groups Helps Them Survive in Iraq," *NYT*, December 2, 2005; Dexter Filkins, "In Shadows, Armed Groups Propel Iraq toward Chaos," *NYT*, May 24, 2006; Nina Kemp, Michael O'Hanlon, and Amy Unikewicz, "The State of Iraq: An Update," *NYT*, June 16, 2006; Nina Kemp, Michael O'Hanlon, and Amy Unikewicz, "The State of Iraq: An Update," *NYT*, March 13, 2007.

2   Wolf Blitzer interview with Lt. Gen. Ricardo Sanchez, CNN, July 27, 2003; "'Bring 'Em on' Fetches Trouble," CBS/AP, July 3, 2003.

3   Cordesman, *Iraq's Evolving Insurgency*; Ned Parker, "The Conflict in Iraq: Saudi Role in Conflict," *Los Angeles Times*, July 15, 2007.

4   Cordesman, *Iraq's Evolving Insurgency*; Ned Parker, "The Conflict in Iraq: Saudi Role in Conflict," *Los Angeles Times*, July 15, 2007.

5   Jessica Stern, "How America Created a Terrorist Haven," *NYT*, August 20, 2003.

6   Sebastian Rotella, "A Road to Ansar began in Italy: Wiretaps Are Said to Show How al-Qaeda Sought to Create in Northern Iraq a Substitute for Training Camps in Afghanistan," *Los Angeles Times*, April 28, 2003.

7   David Kilcullen, "Countering Global Insurgency," *Journal of Strategic Studies* 28, no. 4 (2005): 597–617, Appendix C, 1–2.

CHAPTER 17: ABU GHRAIB, HEARTS, AND MINDS

1 Woodward, *State of Denial*, 266.

2 Ibid., 261.

3 Ibid., 325.

4 "Iraqi Security," *NYT*, May 24, 2005; Michael Moss and David Rodhe, "Misjudgments Marred U.S. Plans for Iraqi Police," *NYT*, May 21, 2006; Kemp, O'Hanlon, and Unikewicz, "The State of Iraq: An Update," March 13, 2007.

5 Woodward, *State of Denial*, 254–55.

6 Stephen Eisenman, *The Abu Ghraib Effect* (New York: Reaktion Books, 2007); Christopher Graveline and Michael Clemens, *The Secrets of Abu Ghraib Revealed: American Soldiers on Trial* (Washington, D.C.: Potomac Books, 2010).

7 Neil Lewis, "Red Cross Found Abuses at Abu Ghraib Last Year," *NYT*, May 11, 2004; Neil Lewis, "Red Cross Says That for Months It Complained of Iraqi Prisoner Abuses to the U.S.," *NYT*, May 7, 2004.

8 Amit Paley, "Most Iraqis Favor Immediate U.S. Pullout, Polls Show," *Washington Post*, September 27, 2006; Pew Institute Survey, various years, http://people-press.org/.

9 Michael Walzer, *Just and Unjust Wars: A Moral Argument with Historical Illustrations* (New York: Basic Books, 2000).

10 Ibid.; Colin Flint and Ghazi-Walid Falah, "How the United States Justified Its War on Terrorism: Prime Morality and the Construction of a 'Just War,'" *Third World Quarterly* 25, no. 8 (2004): 1379–99.

11 Patrick Tyler, "U.N. Chief Ignites Firestorm by Calling Iraq War Illegal," *NYT*, September 17, 2004.

12 Steven Kull, Clay Ramsay, and Evan Lewis, "Misperceptions, the Media, and the Iraq War," *Political Science Quarterly* 118 (Winter 2003–2004): 575.

13 Brigette Nacos, *Terrorism and Counterterrorism: Understanding Threats and Responses in the Post-9/11 World* (New York: Penguin, 2006), 277.

14 John Mueller, "The Iraq Syndrome," *Foreign Affairs* 84, no. 6 (November–December 2005): 49, 44–54.

15 Gary Jacobson, *A Divider, Not a Uniter: George W. Bush and the American People* (New York: Pearson Longman, 2007).

CHAPTER 18: THE SURGE

1 James Baker, Lee Hamilton et al., *The Iraq Study Group Report: The Way Forward: A New Approach* (New York: Vintage, 2006); David Sanger, "Panel Urges Basic Shift in U.S. Policy in Iraq," *NYT*, December 7, 2006; "A Blueprint of a Different Course," *NYT*, December 7, 2006.

2 Thom Shanker, "New Lessons for the Army on Iraq Duty," *NYT*, February 19, 2009; "Poll: Iraqis Pessimistic About War's Outcome," MSNBC, March 2007, http://www.msnbc.msn.com/id/1768430/.

3 For the best book to date on Petraeus, see Linda Robinson, *Tell Me How This Ends: General David Petraeus and the Search for a Way Out of Iraq* (New York: Public Affairs, 2008).

4 Thom Shanker, "U.S. Plans Afghan Effort to Thwart Road Bombs," *NYT*, February 26, 2009.

5 Robinson, *Tell Me How This Ends*, 272.

CHAPTER 19: EMPOWERING IRAN

1   Lawrence Potter and Gary Sick, *Iran, Iraq, and the Legacies of War* (New York: Palgrave Macmillan, 2006); Philip Wolny, *Iran and Iraq: Religion, War, and Geopolitics* (New York: Rosen Publishing, 2009).

2   Rod Norland, "Iran Plays Host to Delegations after Iraq Vote," *NYT*, April 2, 2010.

3   Peter Finn, "Al Qaeda Deputies Harbored by Iran: Pair Are Plotting Attacks, Sources Say," *Washington Post*, August 28, 2002; Jonathan Karl, "Exclusive: Iran in Secret Talks with al-Qaeda, Officials Say," ABC News, May 29, 2008.

4   Nacos, *Terrorism and Counterterrorism*, 109–11.

5   Robert Ebel, *The Geopolitics of Iran's Nuclear Program: But Oil and Gas Still Matter* (Washington, D.C.: Center for Strategic and International Studies, 2010); Bryan Hamilton, *Taming Tehran: An Analysis of U.S. Policies Targeting Iran's Nuclear Program* (New York: Academic Publishers, 2011).

6   Kim Murphy, "U.S. Puts the Squeeze on Iran's Oil Fields," *Los Angeles Times*, January 7, 2007.

7   Helene Cooper and David Sanger, "Obama's Positive Message to Iran Is an Opening Bid in a Diplomatic Drive," *NYT*, March 21, 2009.

CHAPTER 20: WINNERS AND LOSERS

1   Larry Diamond, "What Went Wrong in Iraq," *Foreign Affairs* 83, no. 5 (September– October 2004): 35.

2   Stern, "How America Created a Terrorist Haven"; Peter Bergen and Paul Cruikshank, "The Iraq Effect," *Mother Jones*, March 1, 2007; "Prospects for Iraq's Stability: A Challenging Road Ahead," Iraq National Intelligence Estimate, unclassified version released February 2, 2007.

3   Ivanovich, "Contractor Deaths up 17 Percent."

4   Secretary of Defense Interview with Bob Woodward, October 23, 2003, Department of Defense, News Transcript, April 19, 2004, www.defense.gov/today/default.aspx?showdate=4/19/2004.

5   List of Insurgents Killed in Iraq, Nationmaster, nationmaster.com; Jim Michaels, "Thousands of Enemy Reported Killed," *USA Today*, September 27, 2007.

6   Iraq Index, Brookings Institute, Saban Center for Middle East Policy, http://brookings.edu/saban/iraq-index.aspx.

7   Iraq Body Count, www.iraqbodycount.org.

8   "Humanitarian Situation Report, Sadr City," UN High Commissioner for Refugees, April 12, 2008.

9   Terri Judd, "Barbaric 'Honor Killings' Become the Weapon to Subjugate Women in Iraq," *The Independent*, April 28, 2008.

10 Gordon Adams and Nigel Holmes, "The Price of War," *NYT*, June 28, 2004; Bilmes and Stiglitz, *Three Trillion Dollar War*.

CHAPTER 21: THE FUTURE OF IRAQ

1   "Iraq War Results & Statistics," January 4, 2009, About.com.

2   Timothy Williams, "Departing U.S. Ambassador Warns against Quick Withdrawal from Iraq," NYT, January 22, 2009.

3   Heiko Flottau, "Iraq's Oil Industry in Crisis," ISN Security Watch, December 7, 2005.

4   Michael E. O'Hanlon and Kenneth M. Pollack, "Iraq's Year of Living Dangerously," NYT, February 26, 2009.

5   C.I.A. World Factbook, https://www.cia.gov/library/publications/the-world-factbook/index/html; Nationmaster; Johns Hopkins Bloomberg Public Health Newsletter, October 20, 2006; Sabrina Tavenise and Donald McNeil, "Iraq Dead May Total 600,000," NYT, October 12, 2006; NYT, November 25, 2006; Kemp, Hanlon, and Unkiewicz, "The State of Iraq: An Update," March 13, 2007.

6   Marc Santora and Alan Cowell, "With Swipe at U.S., Iraq Builds Ties to French," NYT, February 11, 2009.

7   Thomas Friedman, "Bush's Iraq Gamble," IHT, March 3, 2003.

8   John Burns and Kirk Semple, "Iraqi Insurgency Has Funds to Sustain Itself," NYT, November 25, 2006.

9   Walter Gibbs, "Scowcroft Urges Wide Role for U.N. in Postwar Iraq," NYT, April 9, 2003.

CHAPTER 22: EXCUSES AND REASONS

1   Douglas Jehl, "Pentagon Reportedly Skewed CIA's View of Qaeda Ties," NYT, October 22, 2004; "How to Skew Intelligence," NYT, October 23, 2004; Mark Mazzetti, "Prewar Intelligence Ignored, Former C.I.A. Official Says," NYT, April 22, 2006.

2   Joseph Wilson, "What I Did Not Find in Iraq," NYT, July 6, 2003.

3   Joseph Wilson, The Politics of Truth: Inside the Lies that Led to War and Betrayed my Wife's CIA Identity: A Diplomat's Memoir (New York: Carroll & Graf, 2004); Douglas Jehl, "Iraq Arms Critics Reacts to Report on Wife," NYT, August 8, 2003; Eric Lichtblau and Richard Bernstein, "White House Denies a Top Aide Identified an Officer of the CIA," NYT, September 30, 2003.

4   Woodward, Plan of Attack; David Sanger, "Bush Reports No Evidence of Hussein Tie to 9/11," NYT, September 18, 2003; Richard Stevenson, "Remember 'Weapons of Mass Destruction'? For Bush They Are Not an Issue," NYT, December 18, 2003.

5   All the biographies of George W. Bush explore his tormented psyche, but for the most explicit analyses, see Justin Frank, Bush on the Couch: Inside the Mind of the President (New York: Harper, 2007), and Dan P. McAdams, George W. Bush and the Redemptive Dream: A Psychological Portrait (New York: Oxford University Press, 2010).

Selected Bibliography

Bamford, James. *A Pretext for War: 9/11, Iraq, and the Abuse of America's Intelligence Agencies*. New York: Anchor Books, 2005.

Chandrasekaran, Rajiv. *Imperial Life in the Emerald City: Inside Iraq's Green Zone*. New York: Knopf, 2006.

Diamond, Larry. *Squandered Victory: The American Occupation and the Bungled Effort to Bring Democracy to Iraq*. New York: Knopf, 2005.

Fawn, Rick, and Raymond Hinnebusch, eds. *The Iraq War: Causes and Consequences*. Boulder, CO: Lynne Rienner, 2006.

Galbraith, Peter W. *The End of Iraq: How American Incompetence Created a War without End*. New York: Simon & Schuster, 2006.

————. *Unintended Consequences: How the War in Iraq Strengthened America's Enemies*. New York: Simon & Schuster, 2008.

Gordon, Michael, and Bernard Trainor. *Cobra II: The Inside Story of the Invasion and Occupation of Iraq*. New York: Knopf, 2005.

Isikoff, Michael, and David Korn. *Hubris: The Inside Story of Spin, Scandal, and the Selling of the Iraq War*. New York: Crown, 2006.

McAdams, Dan P. *George W. Bush and the Redemptive Dream: A Psychological Portrait*. New York: Oxford University Press, 2010.

Miller, F. Christian. *Blood Money: A Story of Wasted Billions, Lost Lives, and Corporate Greed in Iraq*. New York: Little, Brown, 2006.

Packer, George. *The Assassin's Gate: America in Iraq*. New York: Farrar, Straus & Giroux, 2006.

Pearson, Graham S. *The Search for Iraq's Weapons of Mass Destruction: Inspection, Verification, and Non-Proliferation*. New York: Palgrave Macmillan, 2005.

Purham, Todd. *A Time of Our Choosing: America's War in Iraq*. New York: New York Times Books, 2004.

Ricks, Thomas. *Fiasco: The American Military Adventure in Iraq*. New York: Penguin, 2006.

Ritchie, Nick, and Paul Rogers. *The Political Road to War: Bush, 9/11, and the Drive to Overthrow Saddam Hussein*. London: Routledge, 2006.

Sifry, Micah L., and Christopher Cerf, eds. *The Iraq War Reader: History, Documents, Opinions*. New York: Touchstone, 2003.

Woodward, Bob. *Plan of Attack*. New York: Simon & Schuster, 2004.

———. *State of Denial: Bush at War, Part III*. New York: Simon & Schuster, 2006.

———. *The War Within: A Secret White House History*. New York: Simon & Schuster, 2008.

Index

About the Author

William Nester is a professor in the Department of Government and Politics at St. John's University in New York. He is the author of twenty-five previous books on different aspects of international relations.